BIG MEDIA & INTERNET TITANS

BIG MEDIA & INTERNET TITANS
Media Ownership: The Democratic Challenge

EDITED BY
Granville Williams

CAMPAIGN FOR PRESS & BROADCASTING FREEDOM
2014

Big Media & Internet Titans
Media Ownership: the Democratic Challenge
Edited by Granville Williams
Published by the Campaign for Press & Broadcasting Freedom 2014

www.cpbf.org.uk

ISBN: 978-1-898240-07-5

Design and Production Roger Huddle
Printed by Russell Press, Nottingham

A catalogue record for this book is available from the British Library

Contents

Preface • 7

Rupert Murdoch was in triumphalist mood when he launched his Sky Multi-Channel package in September 1993, and contemptuous of any attempts to curb media ownership. "A Labour government isn't going to do anything about it; the sting has gone out of it," he accurately predicted.

Since then, for over 20 years, powered by media lobbying and government deregulation, concentration in media ownership has pushed ahead locally, regionally, nationally and globally.

On 10 November 2006 the cable, broadband and mobile phone company, NTL (now Virgin Media and part of John Malone's Liberty Global's cable tv empire), announced it wanted to buy ITV for £4.7 billion. A week later, just after the markets closed on 17 November, BSkyB announced that it had paid £940 million to acquire a 17.9 per cent stake in ITV. BSkyB said the shock purchase was a move designed to support ITV at a time when its share price was under pressure and it was without a chief executive. In fact it was a spoiler to (successfully) scupper NTL's ambition to merge with ITV and create a rival to BSkyB.

BSkyB's action triggered angry media comments, but silence from the two main political parties. After Ofcom and Office of Fair Trading scrutiny of the share acquisition, Alistair Darling, the Secretary of State for Trade and Industry, referred BSkyB's 17.9% stake in ITV to the Competition Commission in May 2007.

This was a rare example of government intervention against Rupert Murdoch's media empire, made possible only by determined lobbying during the draft Communications Bill which led to a 'public interest test' in the Communications Act of 2003 to scrutinise the democratic consequences of media mergers or takeovers.

The outcome in January 2010, after four challenges by BSkyB, was that the Court of Appeal upheld the Competition Commission's 2007 judgement that Sky must reduce its 17.9per cent stake to below 7.5per cent because it had too much influence over ITV.

These events spurred the Campaign for Press and Broadcasting Freedom (CPBF) to set up the Media Ownership in the Age of Convergence project. We were successful in obtaining funds for our work from the Open Society Foundation and the General Political Fund of the public service union, Unison. This financial support, for which we are extremely grateful, has enabled us to organise conferences, produce pamphlets and respond to a plethora of consultations from government and regulatory bodies. This book is the final product from that project.

The incredible developments since we started the project (News Corporation's plan to take full control of BSkyB, the phone-hacking scandal and trials, the Leveson Inquiry and Report) have underlined how vital the issue of diverse media ownership is for democratic societies, and how excessive media power can be corrosive for journalism and politics.

As this book went to press in May 2014, BSkyB announced an £8.3 billion plan to take full control of its sister companies Sky Italia and Sky Deutschland. At the moment Murdoch holds a 39 per cent stake in BSkyB, while

Fox holds 57 per cent of Sky Deutschland and 100 per cent of Sky Italia. The *Financial Times* commented that the action has 'the feel of a Murdoch master plan. He may want to unify the European TV companies, then bid for the rest of BSkyB itself'.

Media ownership has been a key concern of the CPBF since it was set up in 1979. These are different times and this book, written in a media environment shaped by the internet, is the latest expression of that concern. I think the distinctive contributions by the various authors illuminate this important topic, and I am very grateful to them for their efforts.

I want to thank the CPBF National Council, and particularly Tim Gopsill, for his advice on the book's structure, help with contributors, and the ITV chapter title. Thanks also to Roger Huddle for his work on the design and printing of the book, and to my wife, Sue, for her invaluable proofreading support.

Granville Williams May 2014
Project Director, Media Ownership in
the Age of Convergence

Media ownership: Democratic challenges
Granville Williams

Back to the Future

In 1951, aged 20, Rupert Murdoch was in his first year at Worcester College Oxford with a bust of Lenin on the mantelpiece of his college room. The media landscape has been totally transformed since the 1950s, not only physically, but also in terms of communication technology and the rise of the internet, changes in media ownership structures and the growth of global media groups. Murdoch was later to play a key role in that transformation.

A copy of the *Fleet Street Annual* for 1951, edited by Harold Herd, and picked up from a place whose existence is itself under threat these days – a second-hand bookshop – vividly demonstrates the media world which existed before this transformation. (1)

A souvenir black and white photographic supplement of 'Fleet Street at Mid-Century' reveals the confident bold architecture of Lord Camrose's *Daily Telegraph* and Lord Beaverbrook's *Daily Express* buildings which dominated the north side of Fleet Street and reminds us that it was still the era of the 'press barons'. In 1930 Lord Beaverbrook intervened directly in British politics and estab-

lished the United Empire Party with the support of Lord
Rothermere's *Daily Mail* group. For 19 months the newspapers of the two press barons promoted the new party's
candidates and denigrated the leadership of prime minister Stanley Baldwin. In the St George's Westminster by-
election of March 1931 Baldwin made the 'press dictator-
ship' the election issue. In a powerful speech on 17 March
1931, which still resonates today, he said the newspapers of
Beaverbrook and Rothermere:

> ...are engines of propaganda...Their methods are
> direct falsehood, misrepresentation, half-truths, the
> alteration of the speaker's meaning by putting
> sentences apart from the context, suppression, and
> editorial criticism of speeches which are not reported
> in the paper...What the proprietorship of these papers
> is aiming at is power, but power without responsibility
> – the prerogative of the harlot throughout the ages. (2)

This type of sensational journalism, often produced
under proprietorial pressure, led the National Union of
Journalists (NUJ) to draw up a Code of Professional Conduct at its 1936 Annual Delegate Meeting. Concerns about
the propaganda power of the press barons emerged again
after the sweeping 1945 Labour election victory. In July
1946 the Attorney General, Hartley Shawcross, attacked
the newspaper proprietors:

> They distort the facts, they suppress the news upon
> which free opinions could be freely formed. A small
> handful of newspaper proprietors because of their
> political views, their financial interests, their
> advertisement revenues and so forth are terrified of
> the advent of socialism in this country and are
> determined that the Labour government shall not be
> given a fair run.

This view was echoed by the NUJ. In the same month,
its general secretary, Clem Bundock, proposed the idea of
a royal commission on the press, arguing: 'the freedom of

the press must not be choked by the concentration of newspapers into the hands of two or three powerful commercial groups'. (3)

The Royal Commission on the Press and its report in June 1949 was the first of many attempts to grapple with the core policy issues of newspaper ownership and press regulation, the latest of which was the Leveson Inquiry and the November 2012 Report.(4) The former *Sunday Times* editor, Harold Evans, pointed to one crucial gap in the report and made the links between politics, media power and democracy:

> The biggest disappointment in Leveson is how far he skates over the crucial issue of ownership. It matters very much that the law on competition was broken by Margaret Thatcher's participation in 1981 in a secret deal by which Times Newspapers came under News International's control. All Leveson's fine language in his report about the need for future transparency is justified by the vaguest of references to what made it necessary in the first place. It surely matters a great deal that the greatest concentration of the British press was achieved by a backroom deal that gave News International such sway over British public life. (5)

The press barons of the mid-twentieth century had a specific focus on national politics, but by the time Rupert Murdoch had created his global media group, News Corporation, his media empire was a powerful platform to project his worldview. A particularly frightening example of the depth of Murdoch's influence on world politics was his role in setting the stage for the invasion of Iraq in 2003.

The rapturous support of the Murdoch press for the Iraq war immediately prior to the invasion has been well documented. All of his 175 newspapers supported the war. Murdoch has a clear political vision. He champions anti-statist neoliberal capitalism. He is vehemently opposed to trade union influence and regards himself as locked in a

13

battle against established liberal elites. The corrosive influence of media power, the extraordinary concentration of the press in a small number of hands and the enormous political power that the owners wield, as epitomised by Murdoch, is one of the themes we analyse in this book.

Many of the Fleet Street buildings displayed in the *Annual*'s photographic supplement remain, or in some cases their edifices, but the newspapers which inhabited them have decamped to the Isle of Dogs, Canary Wharf or Blackfriars. Effectively from January 1986, with the move to Wapping of Rupert Murdoch's News International titles, the foundations of the Fleet Street newspaper industry were knocked away. Some have decamped again with, for example, News Corporation selling its Wapping headquarters and bringing its newspapers, the publisher HarperCollins and the news wire service Dow Jones all under one roof near London Bridge station.

There are advertisements in the *Annual* for Monotype Super Casters, Linotypes and Autoplates, and at the back of the book ones for 'fast and accurate typewriting and duplicating services'. These means of creating and communicating information have long since disappeared. The only place you are likely to see Linotypes today is in museums, yet the hot metal technology of the Linotype – lines of text cast in lead – was central to printing in the mid-twentieth century with thousands of the machines in use throughout the world. They speeded up printing by mechanising the process of setting type. Before its invention, typesetting was a time-consuming process done by hand and a major production bottleneck. The explosion of printing in the early twentieth century created jobs for highly-skilled specialists on the Linotype.

Photo typesetting technology began to overtake the Linotype in the early 1950s, and by the 1970s the Linotype was no longer state-of-the-art. Newspaper owners were involved in bitter disputes with printers (typographers in the USA) over the introduction of new computerised typesetting technology. In 1962-63 seven New York City newspapers were closed down in a strike lasting 114 days; in the UK the presses at *The Times* and *The Sunday Times* were at a standstill from November 1978 to November 1979 over the introduction of new technology, and Rupert Murdoch provoked a year-long strike when he sacked 6000 print workers and moved his newspapers to Wapping in January 1986.

Twenty pages in the *Annual* list the names and addresses of British publishers, with a brief indication of their interests, for prospective writers. Some are small scale, specialist publishers, but in amongst them are the most important mid-twentieth century British publishers: W.H.Allen, Jonathan Cape, Victor Gollancz, Heinemann, Hodder and Stoughton, Secker and Warburg, Weidenfeld and Nicolson. None of these exists independently today. W.H Allen, Jonathan Cape, Heinemann, and Secker and Warburg are now part of Random House, the publishing division of the privately-owned global media group Bertelsmann. Victor Gollancz, Weidenfeld and Nicolson, and Hodder and Stoughton are now part of Hachette, the publishing arm of the French Groupe Lagardère.

The *Fleet Street Annual*'s editor, Harold Herd, also wrote a standard history of journalism, *The March of Journalism*, published by George Allen and Unwin in 1952. The publisher, established in 1871, survived as an independent until 1986 when it amalgamated with Bell and Hyman to become Unwin Hyman. It was sold to HarperCollins, the publishing division of Rupert Murdoch's News Corporation, in 1990.

HarperCollins acquired the publishing rights to *The Hobbit* and its sequel, the trilogy, *The Lord of the Rings*, when it bought Unwin Hyman in 1990. *The Hobbit* was first published in 1937 with a very modest 1,500-copy print run. When Tolkien delivered *The Lord of the Rings* manuscript, newsprint and paper were still rationed and the publisher decided to publish the book in three volumes: *The Fellowship of the Rings* in August 1954, *The Two Towers* in November 1954 and *The Return of the King* in October 1955. J.R.R. Tolkien signed a deal which included 50/50 profit-sharing with the publisher. Since then, *The Lord of the Rings* has gone on, according to a 2007 estimate, to sell 150 million copies in more than 50 languages.

Tolkien sold the film and merchandising rights to United Artists in 1967 and they were then sold on by United Artists to Saul Zaentz in 1976. His company, Tolkien Enterprises, granted a licence to New Line Cinema to film the trilogy.

Three films based on *The Lord of the Rings* trilogy were released by New Line Cinema, a division of Time Warner, between 2001 and 2004. A further three motion pictures based on *The Hobbit* have now been released. Time Warner is the third largest global media group with interests spanning film, television, magazine publishing and cable TV. The deal with Tolkien Enterprises meant that New Line also received a licence to develop merchandise based on depictions of the characters in the three films. The revenues from the films and merchandising have been boosted by the synergies which the global media group utilises to cross-promote them.

Box office revenues for the Rings trilogy were nearly $3 billion, merchandise up to $1.2 billion and sales of videos and DVDs another $1.3 billion. The financial scale and commercial complexity of this global media project contrasts dramatically with the modest scope of the mid-twentieth century media world in which the books were first published.

The huge revenues generated by the film trilogy also sparked fierce legal battles over copyright issues. Just weeks before the release of *The Hobbit* in November 2012, an $80 million lawsuit by the Tolkien estate and its book publisher HarperCollins was filed against Time Warner, its New Line subsidiary and the Rings/Hobbit rights holder Saul Zaentz claiming they had infringed the copyright of the books and breached a contract. The crux of the suit was the estate's contention that the original rights agreement entitled the studio to create only 'tangible' merchandise based on the books, not an 'online slot machine' or other digital exploitations that the estate calls 'highly offensive'. (6)

This dispute highlights key issues analysed in this book: the battle between different sections of global corporate media to control creative content and copyright, and the commercialisation of creative works and their transformation, through a variety of 'spin-offs', into cash-generating vehicles. Warner Brothers, as an American corporation owned by its parent company Time Warner, has only one mission: maximise profits for stock holders. If creating Lord of the Rings-themed slot machines means higher profits, there is very little that would hold back a publicly traded entertainment company from producing slot machines, even if this was not in the scope of the original rights deal, until they are challenged by the owners of the original rights in expensive legal battles.

Apart from one advert for Barker, Drabble & Co ('Publicity that grips the mind of millions'), there is a total absence in the *Annual* of the marketing, advertising and PR sectors which now play such enormous economic and political roles in shaping contemporary media and politics. Commercial television was still four years away and in the campaign for it we saw for the first time media policy being shaped by a group of what today we call lobbyists but back then a 'pressure group'. A group of back bench Tory MPs, with the aid of radio and television manufacturers and advertising interests, operating under the umbrella of the Popular Television Association, were able to overcome opposition within their own party and on 30 July 1954 the bill creating the Independent Television Authority became law, ending the monopoly the BBC had sustained for 27 years. (7) Since then a key factor in the formation of media policy in the UK, Europe and the USA has been the role of powerful media groups lobbying governments to persuade them to adopt deregulatory policies and tear up media ownership rules. The Prime Minister, David Cameron, worked in this role as Director of Corporate Communication at Carlton Television from 1994-2001 where his job was to defend the indefensible in terms of the terrible quality of the programmes transmitted by Carlton (they didn't make them) and to lobby the government to allow ITV consolidation. (8)

The *Fleet Street Annual* conjures up a frozen-in-time media world, still constrained by austerity and newsprint rationing, but one on the cusp of tremendous change. The Festival of Britain which opened in May 1951, with its emphasis on modernity and innovation, symbolised the transition, but the horizons of that distant world were still mainly local, regional, national – not global – and it was all about to change utterly. This book focuses on key policy issues around media ownership carried over from the last century, but also on new ones which have emerged in the 21st century.

Future Imperfect:
Internet Giants and Media Consolidation

One such issue is the globalising power of the internet and the web, and, linked to this, the growth of hugely powerful online companies like Amazon, Google and Facebook. The contradiction is that the internet, created by government and run on open source software, and the web devised by Tim Berners-Lee, are free and open, but the internet companies that have grown through exploiting the facilities offered by the free foundation of the web behave in ways which urgently require scrutiny. Big phone and cable companies also want to turn the open network into their private fiefdoms by fiercely resisting the policy of net neutrality and take away many of the freedoms Internet users now take for granted.

John Naughton captures the essential nature of these 'giants of cyberspace' with their clever PR camouflages. "Up to now," he writes, "they have succeeded in branding themselves as different in important ways from the bad old industrial behemoths of the past. Google has its much-vaunted 'don't be evil' slogan...Facebook just wants to help everyone to hook up to 'share' and 'like' stuff...Amazon is fanatically committed to the philosophy that you – the customer – are always right. And so on."

In fact, he argues, these companies are just as ruthless as the corporations from the Gilded Age in the United States:

> They exist to create wealth – vast quantities of it – for their founders and shareholders. Their imperative is to grow and achieve dominance in their chosen markets – as well as in others they now deem to be within their reach. They are as hostile to trade unions, taxation and regulation as John D Rockefeller, JP Morgan and Andrew Carnegie ever were in their day. The only difference is that the new titans employ far fewer people, enjoy higher margins and are less harassed by governments than their predecessors. (9)

But the growth of the internet and these huge online companies has spurred established global media groups and politicians who have their ear to argue that long-established rules on media ownership are outdated. In Australia, one of the most concentrated media markets in the world, the Communications Minister, Malcolm Turnbull, wants to tear up the media ownership rules. He says, "The arrival of the internet and the additional diversity and avenues for competition that it brings really says we should have less regulation and more freedom." This is the oft-repeated neo-liberal argument that the internet will set us free by giving us more news to consume, more diversity, more of everything. The contention is that the internet will disrupt power structures and neutralise traditional gatekeepers, but the reality is very different. The most-visited news websites in Europe, Britain, the US and Australia are the websites of the dominant national news organisations. News aggregation sites on social media are simply reproducing the news stories from these sources and, far from creating different, more diverse sources of news, reinforce the mainstream news agenda.

In the USA we see the pernicious consequences of relentless media consolidation. In January 2011 the Federal Communications Commission (FCC) voted 4-1 to approve the controversial Comcast-NBC Universal merger. It was one of the largest media mergers in history and took place in spite of pledges by Barack Obama during his first presidential campaign to oppose greater media consolidation. Josh Silver of the US media reform group Free Press commented on the FCC decision:

> This deal will give Comcast unprecedented control over both media content and the physical network that delivers it...Such power concentrated in the hands of a single company is deeply troubling. Access to information from a variety of independent sources is essential to an informed citizenry and a functioning democracy.

One of the Commissioners who voted for the merger was Meredith Attwell Baker, on the FCC from 2009 to 2011. She resigned her FCC commission seat and went to work for Comcast, boosting its lobbying power in Washington as senior vice president for governmental affairs just four months after voting to approve the merger. The company spent $18.8 million on lobbying in 2013 and Baker joined 106 other lobbyists, 86 of whom worked in government, before lobbying for Comcast.

In February 2014 Comcast announced its intention, in a $45 billion dollar deal, to buy Time Warner Cable, joining together the largest and second-largest cable and broadband providers in the USA. The announcement provoked a strong response: "The proposed merger of Comcast and Time Warner Cable into a telecommunications behemoth is the media equivalent of 'too big to fail' banking... With its dominance of communications in population centers, its networks and its defining role in digital communications (as a prime provider of Internet service), a single corporation will be in an unprecedented position to dictate the development and character of media content for decades to come." (10)

Who controls the media, and how such power and influence is deployed, goes right to the heart of how democracies function. That was powerfully revealed at the time of the phone-hacking scandal and Rupert Murdoch's bid for BSkyB in the UK. How was Murdoch able to achieve such vast media power, a power which penetrated into politics, the Metropolitan Police and virtually every nook and cranny of public life? That power fostered a belief that Rupert Murdoch's News International was invincible, that its newspapers were immune from ethical restraints and that those who sought to criticise or highlight misdemeanours would themselves be harassed and attacked. Such a situation must not be allowed to reoccur.

We want to ensure that media policy issues are at the centre of policy debate in the run-up to the 2015 general election. That is why the Campaign for Press and Broadcasting Freedom (CPBF) has published this book as part of our work to make questions of media ownership and regulation urgent election issues.

Notes

(1)   *Fleet Street Annual: The Year Book of Journalism and Literary Market Guide*, Fleet Publications, 1951.

(2)   Anne Chisholm and Michael Davie, *Beaverbrook: A Life*, Pimlico, 1993 p305

(3)   The Shawcross and Bundock quotes are from Roy Greenslade, *Press Gang: How Newspapers Make Profits from Propaganda,* Macmillan, 2003, pp 32-33 & p 46

(4)   There were three Royal Commissions on the Press during the 20th century: 1947–1949, 1961–1962 and 1974–1977. In addition there were also the 1972 Younger Committee report on Privacy, the 1990 Calcutt Committee report and 1993 Calcutt Review.

(5)   Harold Evans, 'A clever report but why the silence on media ownership?', *The Guardian*, 29 November 2012.

(6)   Matthew Belloni, 'Tolkien Estate Sues Warner Bros. over Lord of the Rings Slot Machines', *The Hollywood Reporter*, 19 Nov. 2012. Available at: *http://www.hollywoodreporter.com/thr-esq/tolkien-estate-sues-warner-bros-393212*

(7)   H.H.Wilson, *Pressure Group: The Campaign for Commercial Television*, Secker and Warburg, 1961.

(8)   Frances Elliott and James Hanning, *Cameron: The Rise of the New Conservative*, Fourth Estate, 2007

(9)   John Naughton, 'Beware friendly internet giants bearing gifts', *The Observer New Review*, 22 February 2014, p19

(10)   Editorial, 'What's wrong with the Comcast/Time Warner merger?', *The Nation*, 19 February 2014.

The curse of the plcs

Tim Gopsill

The *Surrey Comet* was a big fat weekly paper which had been published since 1854 in Kingston on Thames, one of the most prosperous districts of Britain. That was until the media corporations got their hands on it.

In just two weeks in November 1993 the *Comet* was bought and sold three times, bundled and swapped by marauding media companies jostling to corner the market and establish local monopolies. In the process it was stripped of almost half its journalists and its valuable town centre premises. (1)

The newsroom staff dropped from fifteen to eight. Three reporters were fired by letters delivered to their homes by couriers – the only contact any of the journalists had from the third of the paper's four owners. The National Union of Journalists (NUJ) said its members had been 'traded like slaves'. The office was moved to Twickenham, two miles away, where the Newsquest group that had emerged the ultimate winner had a jumble of other titles.

Now the Comet is owned by a fifth company: the aptly named Gannett Corporation of the USA, which swallowed up Newsquest, one of Britain's biggest regional groups, in 1999. The group also owns the South London Guardian series of free newspapers and the *Richmond and Twickenham Times*, another once-proud former family-owned series, so that particular wealthy quarter of south-west London has been tidied up nicely. The freesheets make up the bulk of the output, and the Comet's sales are currently certified by the Audit Bureau of Circulations at 5,135.

The Surrey story tells as much about proprietorial abuse of ownership of UK media as any amount of trash on daytime TV, racism in the *Daily Express* or persecution of harmless people by the *Daily Mail*. Most of the media may be directed by brutal and reactionary monsters, sure, but that's far from the worst of it. It's not proprietorial whim or political prejudice that is robbing the commercial media of their ability to report the realities of life or present an independent view of them, it is finance.

Not money, but finance. Not private wealth but public corporations. The owners of newspapers, magazines and broadcast stations have always had money and put a good deal of energy into making more, but generally they have operated to an imperative based on some kind of commitment to communicate and comment on the world. The imperative of finance, on the other hand, is to maximise shareholder value. This is not capricious; it is what public limited companies (plcs) do. It is even a legal requirement.

It would be irrelevant and unfair to expect moral or ethical conduct from plcs. There is no reason why they should act benevolently. It is true that many global corporations now like to make a song and dance about 'corporate social responsibility', but that is just public relations. Like the banks with whose business they are so closely intertwined, they are as they are and the only way to contain their activities, if you see the need, is through regulation or the law.

In the later decades of the 1900s and into the 2000s the plcs rampaged through the media sector. The old press barons, running their empires from private wealth or companies, or on the side from other businesses, were mostly swept away. Even the currently most prominent and aggressive proprietors are at the head of public companies: the Murdochs who own four national papers and effectively run Europe's wealthiest broadcaster, BSkyB; the Rothermeres who run the *Daily Mail* group, and the rest – virtually all of them are technically employees as well as shareholders, as were the criminals who happily no longer run the Mirror and Telegraph groups, respectively Robert Maxwell and Conrad Black.

There was a common idea among 20th century media folk that their owners divided into two: those in it for the power or for the money. It was always said, no doubt because they kept saying it themselves, that Lord Beaverbrook, the manic imperialist owner of the Express from the 1930s for nearly 50 years in the mid-20th century, was the archetype of the first; and the urbane but ruthless Lord Thomson of Fleet, owner of the *Times* and other newspapers, the second.

Beaverbrook said: "My purpose was to set up a propaganda paper … and I have never departed from the purpose." Thomson, a salesman by background, defined editorial content as 'the stuff you separate the ads with'. He also coined the phrase 'a licence to print your own money', referring the franchise he won to run Scottish Television. No-one can ever cite others than these two, and in truth neither was quite as single-minded as they liked to make out, but in any case, that was then. There is no question what the plcs' motives might be now.

As *Guardian* reporter Nick Davies wrote in *Flat Earth News*, his incisive look at the way journalism is going, "It would be easier if the essential problem were simply that proprietors were imposing their editorial line on their journalists... As it is we are dealing with a system that is running out of control, with the logic of commerce randomly overwhelming the requirements of reporting." (2)

Whatever happens, they make money

The *Surrey Comet* was exceptional only in the pace of its successive takeovers. In 1996 a third of all local newspapers changed hands, according to research conducted at Cardiff University for *Flat Earth News*. Until that decade there had been up to 20 companies of varying sizes in the field (in addition to the dwindling number of one-paper family firms). By the turn of the century there were four nationwide chains commanding three quarters of the market.

Big city and regional titles with notable pedigrees like the *Yorkshire Post* and the *Birmingham Post & Mail* went through four owners in the 1990s, as did *The Scotsman*, a national paper based in Edinburgh. In Fleet Street – the sobriquet of the area of central London where newspapers were produced for 300 years – exactly the same happened with the Express, Mirror and Telegraph groups, and *The Observer*. All have been subjected, not just to the impulses of bullies, swindlers and crooks, but to market forces as imposed by big corporations.

When things are going well, they roll in money and buy up more assets. When things turn down, they roll in money by stripping assets and slashing away at costs. It has happened in local and national papers, magazines, commercial TV and radio. They have reduced the traditional media to a rump which can no longer meet the standard of providing news and topical material that the public deserves and expects.

The plcs' takeover of the industry in the 1980s coincided with the transformation of the economy by the Conservative government of Margaret Thatcher. That government's fundamental objectives were to direct control of the economy into the hands of private finance, by privatising public assets and running down industrial production, and to break potential resistance through democratic organisations such as trade unions or left-wing local authorities.

The main commercial media were slaveringly enthusiastic about this project; it was a period of shame for the British press, which never before or since has got itself so close to a government. Hardly surprising, considering how well the owners were doing out of it.

One self-evident outcome is the geographical fact that Fleet Street itself no longer exists as a newspaper publishing centre. Like the *Surrey Comet* – and papers all around the country – the nationals lost their offices too. The Street is in the City of London, and in the 1980s that made it hot property.

Widespread financial deregulation, the so-called Big Bang in the City of London, led to rapid growth in the finance industry and the expansion in London of the big global banks and finance houses, which needed big premises. So the opulent Fleet Street headquarters next door to each other of the Express and the Telegraph, architectural marvels of the inter-war years, were converted into the European HQ of Goldman Sachs, the New York merchant bank described as the 'great vampire squid' of banking for its predatory behaviour. Like others, Goldman came to London to take advantage of the lax regulatory regime and it was in these buildings that the great scams were concocted that all but wrecked the western economies 20 years later.

The Mirror building round the corner at the top of Fetter Lane became the headquarters of Sainsbury's supermarkets. The Financial Times building was sold to the Japanese construction giant Obayashi. The rambling buildings of the Murdoch and Mail group papers have been converted to offices for rent or pulled down for speculative development.

As the property market rocketed, this process was repeated all round the country. Local papers used to have often historic and sometimes imposing town centre offices embedded in the community, where people came to tell stories, hand in letters, book small ads or buy copies of photos. Not any more they don't. The plcs have flogged them off. Sometimes they've rented shop premises for ads and editorial but in many places the newsrooms – where there are still local newsrooms – are out on remote industrial estates.

The national papers had better places to move to. Not only could they cash in on their outdated buildings, with their cavernous halls for compositing processes now redundant, but they could get superior accommodation for practically nothing. At that time the extensive docklands of east London – likewise rendered redundant by technology with the adoption of the container trade – were being redeveloped. The corporation set up to co-ordinate the development was offering incentives including the lifting of planning requirements and other regulations.

First to Docklands was Rupert Murdoch's News International, which in 1981 bought a 13.5 acre site in Wapping from Tower Hamlets Council for £1 million – unbelievably cheap. Five years later this was to be the field of the great battle that put the plcs firmly in command of the press. For the media had another tenet of Thatcherism to fulfil: to break the unions.

The technology to convert production from 'hot metal' – literally setting type in molten lead – was widely used in the provincial press and could have been implemented on the nationals a decade earlier, but for a strange alliance, based on mutual interest, between the old patriarchal bosses and the print unions.

Print workers – at least, the skilled compositors who set the metal type – were very highly paid. They enjoyed trade union closed shops throughout the industry and there were many disputes. A complete mythology has been cultivated around the excessive greed and power of the Fleet Street unions, and there were some impressive episodes, but it took two to make such relationships.

Digital technology could make production much cheaper, with much smaller workforces, but the print unions' closed shop meant that competitors would have to pay the rates. No pay, no paper. In other words, it suited the publishers just fine. The old bosses and unions formed a cartel, to protect their power and jobs respectively and keep competitors out of the market.

So much water built up behind the dam that it was bound to burst with great ferocity. Everyone knew what was coming but even so the coup engineered by Rupert Murdoch with the overnight move of his four News International titles to Wapping in January 1986 was a tremendous shock. More than 5,000 workers, manoeuvred into going on strike as a last resort when negotiations got nowhere, were sacked on the spot. (See Ann Field's chapter).

Every single national paper left the Fleet Street area. The *Mirror*, *Telegraph* and *Independent* went to Docklands, where they got peppercorn rental deals in speculative office blocks. No-one needed printing presses in-house anymore, since pages could be transmitted electronically. They either built separate print factories in Docklands (the *Telegraph* and *Express, Guardian, Mail* and *Financial Times*) or printed elsewhere under contract.

These arrangements were lucrative for the companies but disastrous for the press. The Fleet Street journalists' community was smashed to pieces as their offices were thrown to the four winds. For centuries journalists had gathered at the Street's celebrated bars to chew over the topics and stories of the day, and complain about their bosses. The NUJ was strongly represented; union 'chapels', or office branches, were strong enough to look after themselves and spurn the attentions of national officials.

The Fleet Street diaspora put an end to that. Journalists were no longer members of a self-sufficient community with the ability, perhaps limited, to stand together against excesses on the part of their publisher employers. Now they were employees, expected to owe their loyalty not to the profession, nor the public, but to the paper and the company that published it.

NUJ membership declined as the plcs began a process of union derecognition – simply terminating their agreements – around the country. Murdoch, naturally, had done this after Wapping, but so in short order did the Mail and Mirror groups; the union is still excluded at those three companies to this day. Even social links have been snapped. The London Press Club lost its premises in a fire in the 1970s and never got them back. It has had a few temporary homes, and still formally exists as a convenor of black-bowtie-and-dinner-jacket functions for ageing luminaries, but London must be the only capital city in the world without a national press club as the go-to venue for visiting as well as local hacks.

Murdoch's dirty work for others

Another beneficiary of the Big Bang was the venerable Reuters news agency, which had diversified into the business of providing financial information and become fantastically profitable. Their black and green screens sat over every currency, stock and commodity trader's workstation. Even in 1984 the actual provision of news was less than 10 per cent of Reuters' turnover.

Reuters was a non-profit-making trust; its nominal shares were in the hands of UK, Irish, Australian and New Zealand newspaper publishers. The plcs got the lawyers to work and, hey presto, they found the key to float the agency as a plc and unlock capital estimated to have been more than £300 million. The prime mover among the plcs to smash open the traditional structure – against the wishes of some – was reported to have been Trafalgar House, a construction and shipping company headed by Lord Victor Matthews, who had bought the Express group, beating off competition from the *Daily Mail* and two highly dubious business magnates called Tiny Rowland and Sir James Goldsmith. Talk about the race to the bottom! (3)

The terms of the flotation stipulated that the plcs couldn't sell all their shares to cash in straight away, but they soon found ways round it. First to do so was the permanently cash-hungry Robert Maxwell whose company owned the Mirror group. Rupert Murdoch's News Corporation, owner of four national papers that controlled 35 per cent of the market, followed suit. The Reuters windfall, as it became known, was a handy source of funding for the plcs in paying off the redundant printers and re-equipping production.

Once Rupert Murdoch had done their dirty work for them, they were able to get on with some serious profiteering. The performance was staggering. Ever since 1986, newspaper sales have fallen relentlessly, yet profits have soared. Through 20 years of boom and bust the media corporations unremittingly bought up and traded titles, stripped their assets and slashed costs, while the content got thinner and thinner.

Take the Mirror group, which had become the first to be taken over by a non-media company, the papermaking conglomerate Reed International. The group had included IPC Magazines, the biggest and most successful magazine publisher in Britain, which guaranteed financial stability. Reed separated off the magazines into a separate company, and in 1984 put the three titles on the market. Editorial executives wanted to float the papers on their own, to re-establish their independence. Reed went behind their backs and sold to Robert Maxwell, a bully, fraudster and fantasist who had been trying to buy a newspaper for years but everyone else had seen him coming. (Reed itself was taken over by the Dutch giant Elsevier, having sold off its IPC consumer magazines, which include all the big middle-market women's weeklies, to Time Warner of the USA).

But, as anyone who had anything to do with Maxwell could have told them, he wrecked the *Daily Mirror*. He made it a laughing stock by bullying the editors into giving space to his embarrassing self-publicising stunts, then began looting the company, now part of his Maxwell Communications Corporation, to buy its stock to ramp up the share price. Maxwell had amassed a printing and publishing empire on other people's money and everything depended on share price as a sign of creditworthiness. When, after cleaning out the Mirror's pension fund (of more than £400 million), the banks began calling in loans he could not repay, a body said to be Robert Maxwell was found in the sea near the Canary Islands where he had taken his luxury yacht on an impromptu cruise, and Mirror executives were left to clear up the mess.

A consortium of banks led by NatWest swooped on the group, who in turn installed a ruthless management led by David Montgomery, a one-time editor of the *News of the World* who was launching himself on a mission to make media more profitable by slashing away at costs. *The Mirror* gave him the perfect testing ground.

His first act was to fire 100 casual sub-editors overnight: they were literally turned away by security next time they turned up for work. Sackings continued relentlessly. A dozen NUJ reps were sacked and the union derecognised. The staff called Montgomery 'Rommel' – because 'Monty was on our side', but worse was to come.

In 1999 the group was taken over by Trinity International, an aggressive regional publisher based in Liverpool, which was on a takeover binge, buying up Thomson's big regional newspaper group to add to those in Birmingham which Montgomery had bought for £297 million. Trinity Mirror plc became Britain's biggest newspaper publisher in terms of titles – and entered a decade of fantastic profiteering.

Profits from the jaws of loss

The 2000s were supposed to be the decade of doom for the press. The executioner would be the internet, which would first take away all their advertisers, then their readers. The figures were bearing this out. Sales and advertising revenues were falling fast. Everybody was agreed on this, including the publishers, who were adamant that they would never make money from the internet. Why should people pay, it was asked, when they can get free content so easily online?

There is a good answer to that, which is that they will pay if they want it but they won't if it's rubbish, and that is what the publishers had on offer.

As time has gone on publishers have found they can in fact make money from online advertising, and even printed papers have shown surprising resilience. The owners didn't want to know that. The doomsday scenario absolved them of having to work out difficult solutions and allowed them particularly to bully their staffs into accepting rampant closures and massive job cuts. The Cardiff research for Flat Earth News showed that since 1986 half of all the 8,000 journalists on local papers had lost their jobs. And since 2000, more than 100 papers have been closed.

Yet the companies have continually made new acquisitions and turned in impressive profits. Trinity Mirror's operating profits (before tax and various accounting costs) in its first ten years averaged 17.5 per cent – a phenomenal rate – and they weren't even the highest. Newsquest's operating profits for the same period averaged 29.5 per cent, and at the highest of the lot, Johnston Press, it was 30.6 per cent. In the real world, big corporations reckon to be doing well at 5-8 per cent, but this was not the real world. The press owners were determined to extract every penny from their enterprises while the going was good.

They were paying over the odds for more papers to

strip bare. When Newsquest bought Southnews, a small publisher of papers sold off by the other groups in Southern England, in 2000, it paid a 57 per cent premium on the share value: £12 instead of £7.62. Southnews boss Gareth Clark pocketed £23 million. This was not an untypical remuneration in those times. Five directors of Newsquest made £31 million between them when they floated the company in 1997 and a further £29 million when Gannett acquired it two years later.

Conrad Black, the kleptocratic owner of the Telegraph group, was jailed for six and a half years in the USA in 2007 for fraud and stealing from his own company – £223 million according to its own figures. But then all the media bosses think in millions, winning pay and bonuses that often do not appear to relate to performance.

In 2008 Tim Bowdler, CEO of the miracle-working profit machine that is Johnston Press (JP), was awarded a performance-related bonus of £516,000, plus a £172,000 uplift in his pension, making his pot worth £1.3 million. Interestingly, that year was an absolute catastrophe for the company. It had suffered one of the biggest share price crashes in media history, falling by 97 per cent, from 490.5p to 7.1p in a year. JP's market capitalisation of £45 million was now less than a tenth of its debt. Yes, in 2009 it owed £465 million. In 2008 it saw a 15 per cent fall in advertising revenues and cut more than 900 jobs – or 12 per cent of its total workforce. Yet it still returned an operating profit of £128 million, which was still 17.5 per cent of turnover.

Johnston Press is based in Edinburgh, where around the turn of the century someone must have put something in the water that made corporate executives mad. The city's two famous banks – the Bank of Scotland (founded in 1695) and the Royal Bank of Scotland (1797) – threw off three centuries of stability for idiotic speculation that nearly destroyed the British economy. At the same time the equally august Johnston Press (founded

1767) set out on a frenzied campaign of expansion, acting like a football manager on the last day of the transfer window. It ran up vast debts as it borrowed heavily to buy more. By 2008 JP owned 286 newspapers.

The company blew £160 million on Edinburgh's own daily papers, *The Scotsman* and *Evening News*, and a staggering £560 million on the *Yorkshire Post* and associated titles in Leeds. The wackiest purchase was a disparate bunch of 15 weekly papers in Ireland, for which in 2005 it paid an estimated £225 million. In 2008 in a desperate move to claw back some cash it put them on the market, reportedly prepared to accept a third of what it paid. But not even the former owners would buy them back and the offer had to be withdrawn in humiliation. Not until 2014 were they sold – to a British advertising agency chief for £7.2 million.(4) Figures vary according to how you calculate £s and €s at particular times, but it was a loss of over £200 million.

The point about these transactions is that none had anything to do with news, readers, journalists or newspapers in any way. They were about nothing but company finance – share price and profit. JP has no interest in the content of the papers. The same goes for other groups, whether their bosses are also after the power or the kudos or not. Commitments to owning and running media, and to the quality of these media, are not the same thing.

A fit and proper person?

The Express group is currently in the hands of its fifth owners since the 1960s. The Aitken family (Lord Beaverbrook and sons) sold out to Lord (Victor) Matthews' construction group, Trafalgar House, who were ousted by United Newspapers, a regional group headed by accountant Lord (David) Stevens, which in turn lost out to MAI, an asset management company headed by venture capitalist Lord (Clive) Hollick, which in 2000 sold the papers to

Northern and Shell, a private company (not a plc) run by Richard Desmond.

Desmond made his pile from pornography, with a string of sleazy top shelf mags and Television X, a group of adult satellite TV channels. His control of the *Daily Express*, *Sunday Express* and *Daily Star*, plus the celebrity magazine OK! and Channel 5, a licenced terrestrial TV channel, gives him a platform for self-promotion to an embarrassing degree. He's committed to publishing, sure, but his big thing is money.

To establish his respectability, he made a £100,000 donation to Tony Blair's New Labour Party, then in government, which the papers had been swung to support by Lord Hollick. After a couple of years he switched back to the Tories, having, he reportedly said, made a profit because the party spent £114,000 on advertising. (5) Political allegiance to him was a commercial matter.

Desmond bought a new building by the Thames in the City of London and rented it out to his own papers for £7.6 million a year. He evidently has a prodigious talent for making money. In his first four years in control of the *Express*, he paid himself a total of £128 million in salary and pension contributions – more than the £125 million he had paid for the papers. In the same period staff numbers were cut by 23 per cent and the annual wage bill fell from £45 million to £35 million.

Meanwhile the content of the *Daily* and *Sunday Express* has deteriorated so much that sales have more than halved since he bought them (6), and staffing has been slashed to the extent that the journalists' union, the NUJ, has twice staged strikes, and has twice laid formal cases with the Press Complaints Commission against the racism that Desmond imposes on the coverage of immigration.

Desmond's acquisition of Channel 5 in 2010 made a mockery of the UK's regulations on cross-media ownership. The 2003 Communications Act opened up the ownership of the smallest national terrestrial channel, but even so the complete lack of regulatory interest in control passing to the private owner of a chain of papers was extraordinary. He paid its German owners RTL £100 million and certainly made it profitable with a tabloid schedule of police and crime, bolstered by the revival of the near-defunct Big Brother 'reality' format. In 2014 he put it on the market at £700 million and sold it to the US media company Viacom, one of the big five global media groups, for £450 million – another nice earner.

In Desmond's domain, even worse than Channel 5 and the two Expresses is the *Daily Star*, a trashy tabloid 37 launched by Lord Matthews during his tenure of the Express in 1978 to use up downtime on the presses, and extend the market downwards while it was about it. Nine years later, when Lord Stevens had taken control of the group – telling one of his editors: "I loathe and detest ALL journalists" (7) – he tried to take it even further downmarket and ran into trouble.

Stevens did a deal with David Sullivan, another pornographer and owner of the barrel-scraping *Sunday Sport*, to invest in and hand editorial control to Sullivan's company Apollo. Sullivan's editor, Mike Gabbert, described by Express MD Andrew Cameron as 'a gutter rat ... archetypal sleaze journalist ... low-life and utterly immoral', announced his aim to print 'the biggest boobs possible' and began on day one with pix of a girl of 15. (7) It was a disaster. Sales actually went down, staff resigned and complaints soared, but it wasn't outraged MPs or infuriated columnists who brought an abrupt end to the arrangement after just eight weeks; it was supermarket chain Tesco which cancelled £400,000 of advertising.

One of the unsuccessful bidders for the Express group when Desmond bought it was the dreaded David Montgomery, who had run out of road at the Mirror in 1999, forced out by investors as they prepared to sell out to Trinity. In 2004 he had a go at buying the Telegraph group in the aftermath of the Conrad Black calamity, at the head of a consortium of venture capitalists. His pitch was to merge the daily and Sunday titles, sacking most of the latter's staff. (The successful bidders, the peculiar and secretive Barclay twins who run a massive shipping and hotel conglomerate operation from the tax-free base of their own private Channel Island, made do with only 100 sackings to start with, though there were plenty more to come.)

Meanwhile, after running an internet provider in Africa and a broadcasting company in New Zealand, Montgomery fronted an investment fund called Mecom that bought up a dozen insufficiently money-making papers around Europe to sack some staff and goose up the profits a little. In 2011 he was forced out by the big shareholders and began looking round for more media assets to strip and two years later emerged like a ghoul from the grave at the head of another new venture-capitalised company, Local World, which bought out the titles of a number of regional publishers, notably those of the Daily Mail and General Trust (DMGT).

DMGT is a great plc beast in the media jungle. It has hereditary rulers – the Rothermere family – but they spend as well as make money and their national publications and websites are way ahead of the competition in terms of sales, advertising, staffing and profits. But the provincial titles, Northcliffe Media, were lagging behind; in 2012 they had made only £26 million profit, up 53 per cent on the previous year, on sales of £213 million; that is 12 per cent, just below its 13 per cent average since 2000. This was achieved by sacking 324 employees, one in eight of the payroll. It needed a Montgomery to outdo that and no doubt at Local World he will.

He soon declared his intent to subject the group of 16 daily and 76 weekly papers to the kind of treatment that is the shared refrain of 21st century media owners. He told the House of Commons culture committee in 2013 that he wants much of the 'human interface' involved in news publishing to disappear. "Journalists collecting stories one by one is hugely unproductive. They will have to have new skills, greater responsibility for self-publishing on different platforms."

The news industry "cannot sustain a hugely wasteful model from the middle ages," he said, "where a single journalist goes out on a single story, comes back and writes it up." The job of journalists is to "manage content and lots of content that comes from the community itself."

Reporting, in other words, is expensive. User-generated content, as it is known in the business – stuff that comes from the public, from Twitter, blogs and other social media, from self-publicising organisations and individuals, from interns and wannabes, 'citizen journalists' sitting at home with their computers – all that is free. No professional filter is required. Material that comes in, goes in. Owners can get rid of most of the journalists like they got rid of most of the printers 25 years ago.

Little surprise that Johnston Press has become a keen adherent of this strategy. The beleaguered group has taken on as chief executive Ashley Highfield, a former BBC digital executive, who announced in 2014: "Using web-based editorial software the group is now allowing trusted contributors the ability to author content directly." He was reporting continued profits in 2013 of £54.3 million, achieved, he said, by cutting costs. JP axed nearly 1,600 staff in 2012-13 and cut £33.8 million out of its operating costs.

In 2006 the then President of the NUJ, Chris Morley, said the editors of the regional press were "setting upon their titles like vampires in a blood bank. There seems to be no limit to not only thinking the unthinkable, but doing it too – just to shave the profit margins up a little higher... To this end they are dreaming up unthinkable ideas to keep up these extraordinary profit levels."

It is indeed amazing that there are still resources to cut and staff to dispose of on local papers, but it seems there are, and one scheme that holds a particular charm for publishers is called 'hubbing'. This involves closing local offices to move the production of a number of papers in one central location or hub. Its cost-saving appeal is obvious, it has been tried dozens of times, and it never works. When you take journalists out of a community, severing the connections, you take the community out of them. They lose contacts, they miss stories, and colleagues in the hub with no local knowledge are always going to get things wrong.

Yet the publishers persist. In April 2014 Newsquest closed the offices of the *Bromsgrove Advertiser* and *Kidderminster Shuttle* in Worcestershire and transferred the reporters to its office in Stourbridge, West Midlands. But no production is done in Stourbridge; it has already lost its sub-editors to a super-hub in Newport, South Wales, where Newsquest is centralising the production of dozens of papers. Among these, incredibly, are its daily titles in the north of England, in Bradford and Darlington. You will have journalists producing stories for websites and papers in places they have never heard of, let alone been to.

The same month, in London, Trinity Mirror closed the Fulham and Hammersmith Chronicle series, leaving a whole London borough without a newspaper office. Fifteen journalists will be sacked, with staff on other TM papers in west London being moved to a hub in Watford. Indeed, TM has an even more ingenious scheme to do away with offices altogether. Reporters can work remotely, that is, at home, or on the move. The company is doing the same at the *Crewe Chronicle* in Cheshire, and, not missing out, Johnston Press has closed the *Skegness Standard* office in Lincolnshire to make it an 'officeless paper'.

Profits at News International, then the UK subsidiary of Rupert Murdoch's News Corporation, soared after the jobs massacre at Wapping. In 1985, the year before, it made £35.6 million, with a workforce of 8,731. The years 1986-87 themselves were obviously costly, but in 1988 NI made £144.6 profit with a workforce registered at just 949. *The Sun* alone was making £1 million a week.

The money generated by the five titles – *Sun, News of the World, Times, Sunday Times* and *Today* – was to help News Corp launch Sky TV in Europe and Fox in the USA. It is an American company, and not just the Murdochs' family business. In fact the dynasty's long-term position is far from secure.

Major shareholders twice came close to dumping James and Lachlan, the sons of Rupert Murdoch, off the board at the AGMs in 2011-12. They were disgruntled in the aftermath of the *News of the World* scandal, which rocked the establishment in Britain, but in America cost them money. To the corporate monsters who run News Corporation, Rupert's London newspapers are just a troublesome distraction that don't even make serious profits any more – not by their standards.

What really annoyed them was the loss of the bid to take over BskyB. The application to buy up the 61 per cent that News Corporation did not own was well on the way to being nodded through by the UK's new Conservative-led government in 2011 when the scandal broke and within days it collapsed. That was a big setback, and it was only News Corporation's rigged share structure, that gives the Murdoch family 40 per cent of the voting rights, despite owning only 12 per cent of the equity, that saved them.

Even so, 35 per cent voted against James, who as head of News International had been responsible for the NoW catastrophe, and 34 per cent against Lachlan, who ran a TV network in the family's native Australia. Even Chairman Rupert, who has called the shots for more than 50 years, received 14 per cent 'no' votes. This is not what is supposed to happen with media barons. No-one voted against Lord Beaverbrook or accused Lord Thomson of jeopardising profits.

To save their skin, Murdoch decided to split the corporation in two, by hiving off the profitable film and TV interests into a new company called 21st Century Fox. This entity will make most of the money for the shareholders – and, disconnected from the discredited newspapers, could well in quieter times bid again for BSkyB. The damaged News International newspapers in the UK, conveniently rebranded as News UK, stay with News Corp, along with those elsewhere in the world and other publishing operations.

No-one knows how long the shareholders will want to hang on to these rather tarnished assets; spasmodic speculation about a sale is tempered by the realities of the market and the fact that, legally, under the terms of their acquisition by Murdoch, they cannot be broken up. But it would be an almost divine stroke of retribution if News Corp, the mightiest of the UK-related media corporations, turned its back on the Murdochs, who have done more than almost anyone to entrench corporate power.

No money in the internet

It will no doubt be said that newspapers are being overtaken by history. Circulation figures bear out the rapid demise of the local press, and the nationals are in inexorable decline as well. Readers and advertisers are in flight. But this does not absolve their owners of failing in their responsibility to maintain them, because what matters now is the internet. Newspapers are no longer printed matter with a website on the side; they are 24-hour online news operations with a periodical version that appears on paper. And this is the real crime of the media plcs: that they put profiteering above investment when technology was offering rapid change.

Some news websites are doing brilliantly. Some editors in the mid-1990s saw not just that they would have to migrate online, but that there was massive potential for growth and new styles for presenting journalism. Two of the biggest and best serious new sites in the world, the BBC's and *The Guardian's*, started then and have flourished through following coherent strategies.

In April 2014 guardian.com clocked for the first time 100 million unique users a month. Around a third are in the UK and a third in the USA, where there is now a huge Guardian operation. The strategy doggedly followed by editor Alan Rusbridger – in the face of all-round scepticism – has been to maintain free access by developing international traffic, offering a universal slightly left-of-centre slant on world events, and it is pulling in the ads. Digital revenue has doubled in five years to £70 million a year.

The BBC's massively comprehensive site claims 40 million users a week, the long-term result of investment launched by much-maligned Director General John Birt in the 1990s. Its success is matched by the relentlessness of the criticism from commercial media – newspapers as well as commercial TV – for the supposed unfairness inherent in its public funding. They claim it tilts the market against them.

Of course, *The Guardian* and BBC are not owned by plcs (the BBC is funded by the universal licence fee; *The Guardian* is owned by a trust that can plough profits, when it makes them, into investment). But in the 1990s, when these two began their ambitious website programmes, newspaper publishers and TV companies had plenty of cash to invest had they chosen to. They had made enormous savings from the technologies of the 1980s, getting rid of half their payrolls. But they were hamstrung by the short-term demands of finance to maximise shareholder returns, and they couldn't invest in websites because their owners could not see the profit in them.

Nick Davies wrote in *Flat Earth News*: "If these savings were recycled back into newsrooms, we could start to reverse the process which has made the media so vulnerable … So far, media owners have shown every sign of grasping electronic delivery as yet another chance to cut costs and increase revenue without putting anything back into journalism."

The local and national pictures were different. Local papers, which have been devastated by the loss of particularly property and classified advertising, made no attempts to offer cheap or initially free space to draw advertisers to dedicated local sites. As a result, specialist sites sprung up that had no editorial costs to bear and the business was lost forever.

The provincial groups did eventually launch perfunctory sites but these were branded by corporate ownership, not by local title. So Northcliffe's sites were all prefaced 'thisis …'; for example, the Leicester Mercury website was called thisisleicestershire.com. Trinity Mirror's were prefaced 'ic…' as in icliverpool.co.uk for the Liverpool Echo. Johnston Press's were called JohnstonPress/wherever. co.uk. When they belatedly decided to combine forces to offer nationwide advertising between them they called the sites 'fish4…' as in fish4homes.co.uk. These names were presumably dreamt up by moronic and expensive marketing consultants, but readers neither know nor care who owns their local paper, and the emphasis away from the local towards corporate identity was only going to lose their custom.

Ten years too late, in the early years of the 21st century, publishers realised they had to do something more with their websites than just upload the contents of their papers; in effect, to become web publishers with constantly updated news and comment and a daily extract in print on the side. The grim fact was that this required, or should have required, more investment and more journalists than they wanted to pay for.

One by one, *The Telegraph, Financial Times* and *The Independent* developed authoritative rolling news sites and the journalists found themselves having to produce work on the same subject in two or three different media: instantly on the website, more fully in print, commenting in a blog and perhaps a podcast; it was hardly their fault if quality, the range of sources interviewed or consulted and the extent of checking all fell.

The Murdoch press showed a limited understanding of the medium, offering little that was new and then hiding the titles behind a paywall. The company does not publish subscription figures but they are not thought to be high. Some believe that the move was intended to package subscriptions to the sites with TV, internet and mobile phone provision after BSkyB was added to the stable; if so, that was a miscalculation.

The down-market papers displayed have even less interest, offering little more than glamour and gossip, which can hardly compete with the multitude already active in the field – except for one, the extraordinary Mail Online, which has hit on a celebrity-based formula that appears to have little if any relationship to the *Daily Mail* newspaper and is proving a runaway success.

In 2014 Mail Online passed the 200 million monthly browser mark. Its revenues, approaching £60 million a year, are still lower than *The Guardian*'s, but are rising faster than the advertising decline in print. This turnaround, whatever you think of it, comes from the kind of investment that media need. Like *The Guardian*, Mail Online has fast-growing operations in the USA, with offices in New York and Los Angeles, and is said to employ more than 400 'journalists', mostly on compiling that endlessly scrolling right-hand column in which the true celebrity of the individuals whose mundane activities are reported decreases rapidly with length.

It's obvious where the money is. In the market as a whole, online advertising is moving fast towards taking more than 50 per cent of the total; in 2013 it stood at 44.3 per cent, predicted to rise to 47.5 percent in 2014. In printed newspapers the share in 2013 was 15.3 per cent, predicted to fall to 13.8 per cent in 2014. (9) (Broadcasting takes about 27 per cent, magazines about 5 per cent.) In the 20th century all of it went into newspapers, magazines and TV. Just look at the potential revenue the media plcs have thrown away by their failure to invest in the internet.

The consequences of concentrated ownership of the media have tended to be viewed ideologically, in terms of the political and social bias of the owners and the effect of coverage on politics and social groups. For decades there was campaigning against the rigid right-wing anti-labour bias of the Tory Press, yet between 1945 and 1974, when the Labour Party enjoyed the unquestioning support of only one national daily paper, *The Mirror*, it nevertheless won six general elections.

Such considerations pale into insignificance compared with the havoc wrought by the plcs in the 30 years since they supplanted the Tory toffs in control of the press. The corporations have used their market domination to bleed excessive profits, sack staff by the thousand, refuse to invest, deplete their publications of resources and run them into the ground.

Limiting the range and extent of media that a company can control could be a first step to reversing the decline, because companies seek to increase their holdings to create economies of scale – and have lobbied heavily for greater freedom to amass more local monopolies. There are indeed regulations against the concentration of media in local areas, though you might not think so, by making takeovers subject to approval by Office of Fair Trading (OFT) and Competition Commission. The media owners have pressed hard for these to be scrapped, arguing that mergers are the only way to save some local papers. They wanted to be able to swap loss-making titles for others in the same area that they could close down to entrench their monopolies.

In 2009 the OFT responded to the pressure and conducted a review of the regulations, which to the companies' horror decided against relaxation. The plcs do not always get their own way, and campaigns to make the regulations more effective to save titles could get widespread support.

But stopping the rot is not enough. New media have got to grow, free of the stranglehold of the big-money corporations. When a publication, online or print, is insufficiently profitable for the corporations then, rather than bleed it to death, they should have to hand it over to others whose objectives are more socially and communally positive. There are plenty of initiatives of this kind – local, national, niche and specialist. They will have to be supported and funded to supplant the usurpers who have taken over Britain's media.

Notes

1.   *The Journalist*, NUJ, December 1993, p5.

2.   Nick Davies, *Flat Earth News*, Chatto & Windus, 2008.

3.   Roy Greenslade, *Press Gang: How Newspapers Make Profits from Propaganda*, Macmillan, 2003, p 376.

4.   *www.pressgazette.co.uk* April 2 2014.

5.   Fat Cats, *The Journalist,* NUJ April 2003.

6.   According to the Audit Bureau of Circulations, sales of the *Daily Express* in 2000 were 1,050,846, in 2014, 500,473. *Sunday Express* in 2000 974,310⟨, in 2014 430,601.

7.   Greenslade op cit p231.

8.   Greenslade op cit p512; Raymond Snoddy, *The Good, the Bad and the Unacceptable, Hard News about the British Press*, London, 1992, p132.

9.   *http://www.theguardian.com/media/2014/mar/10/uk-mobile-advertising-overtake-newspaper-revenue*, March 10 2014.

The strike that made the modern media

Ann Field

Despite the name given to the national newspaper industry not a single national newspaper or news agency remains in Fleet Street. At least 20,000 people lost their jobs during the general exodus which followed the Wapping dispute in 1986 and several thousand more jobs were shed as a consequence of production changes and regional printing. Trade union agreements which for 100 years had protected workers across all departments from journalists to cleaners were ripped up or watered down to levels of enfeeblement unimaginable previously.

The strike that made the modern media began in response to impossible and threatening demands by Rupert Murdoch's News International. Within minutes of the strike beginning the company started to sack the 5500-strong unionised workforce, moving overnight his entire national newspaper operation to Wapping in east London's former docklands.

Twenty five years later production had been moved again to an area just north of the M25, two national newspapers had been closed by the company and a scandal was uncovered which enveloped Murdoch newspapers, police, politicians and public officials.

The usual narrative and analysis of disputes and strikes charge trade unions with the responsibility for the conflict and any subsequent loss of jobs and conditions. Never was there so much evidence available to the contrary as in the case of the News International dispute in 1986, and so studiously ignored by all and sundry then and ever since.

The national press was triumphant at what they perceived as the crushing of the National Union of Mineworkers. Anti-union hysteria had already reached new peaks during the late 1970s and throughout the early 1980s, justifying the incoming Tory government's programme of putting back workers' trade union rights 70 years. Eddy Shah's Messenger Group of newspapers was among the first to use the so-called Employment Acts of 1980 and 1982 against the NGA (National Graphical Association) and the NUJ (National Union of Journalists) in a bitter dispute at Warrington. Fresh from his victory, and egged on by *Sunday Times* editor Andrew Neil, Shah decided to launch a non-union national newspaper *Today*. (1)

The mineworkers' strike was drawing to a close in the first few months of 1985. At the same time Murdoch and his team were putting the finishing touches to their 'dash for freedom' and the plan to take on the tight-knit community of Fleet Street workers and their unions aided by government, their new legal restrictions on trade unions, their police militia and the rest of the media baying in support.

The company had been plotting a course of action for at least 18 months before the dismissals in January 1986. Former *Sunday Times* Insight journalist Linda Melvern in her book *The End of the Street* published in the last few months of the Wapping dispute describes how the whole project had been planned and executed in utmost secrecy. Even machinery imported from the United States had had the carriage labels stripped off to ensure anonymity, before it was set up in a warehouse in south London and then dismantled and secretly installed in Wapping. (2)

Chapels (workplace union branches) at the Bouverie Street plant just off Fleet Street were angered by the management's apparent withdrawal from talks about agreed re-location to the brand new site at Wapping in east London's former docklands. Anger and suspicions grew during the prolonged silence from early 1985 until the autumn of that year.

News of recruitment of workers for an unnamed major printing company in London began to filter through from trade union friends of the print unions who discovered that the electricians' union, the EETPU, appeared to be acting as a recruiting agent in Southampton and in Glasgow.

The electricians' union had become the main focus for support by government and media. It had fallen under a regime of right-wing business trade unionism. Their officials were touring British industry making deals and signing agreements with any employer who wanted to free themselves from genuine collective bargaining agreements. Binding arbitration, legally binding agreements and no-strike deals were the hallmark of the outcome of an EETPU negotiation. Employers queued to sign them up, depriving thousands of workers of rights and the ability to be represented by an independent trade union. Murdoch chose the EETPU as the vehicle for breaking down genuine and independent trade union organisation.

Having involved and consulted *The Sun* and *News of the World* union reps in the early stages of the purchase of the site and the construction and planning of production areas and machinery, Murdoch decided to ditch the entire workforce and their trade unions. This was not known at the time: all that was known was that the management stopped talking to the chapels about relocation and that their attitude was one of increasing hostility. The hostility generated a similar response by the unions, and relations worsened from the latter half of 1984 onwards.

Some agreements had already been made relating to the

move to Wapping for some departments; draft agreements for others were stifled by management silence or stalled through change of management position. Technology agreements were being made throughout the industry in regional and national newspapers, although not without pain and sometimes conflict where companies sought to reduce unnecessarily heavy job losses or impose reductions in terms and conditions of employment. Despite the worsening atmosphere the expectation remained among most of the workforce and trade union leaders that agreements would be secured for the move to Wapping.

After a silence of six months and refusal to talk, the company suddenly agreed to meet the unions in the autumn of 1985. News International denied allegations they were recruiting new staff recruited for them by the EET-PU, claiming that any staff working on the Wapping site were merely installing and proving machinery and equipment. However, an entirely different agenda was presented by Murdoch's team. Relocation of *The Sun* and *News of the World* would not be discussed. The only item for discussion was a new London evening newspaper – the fictional *London Post*. The management claimed the Wapping site was only being prepared for this new publication and brand new terms and conditions would apply for any staff transferring to Wapping. Murdoch stipulated that negotiations for relocation of *The Sun* and *News of the World* to Wapping would not start unless agreement was reached for production of the new newspaper, and a Christmas deadline was set for compliance. (3)

The unions asked for the management's proposals for employment terms on the new newspaper. A document was issued which included binding arbitration, a legally binding commitment, a no-strike clause and a variety of other mechanisms to ensure that the management would have unfettered rights to hire, fire and manage staff and jobs, terms and conditions with no effective right of negotiation or representation for the workers. Furthermore, the management declared, the document was entirely non-negotiable and an offer to any employee to relocate to Wapping was conditional upon acceptance of these terms.

Given the strength of print union organisation built up over the previous nine decades, it had been inconceivable to most of Murdoch's employees that they would be cast aside or crushed. Yet the realisation was dawning that a terrible dispute was becoming inevitable. Their fears were compounded when the management issued notice of termination of all trade union agreements for employees at *The Sun* and *News of the World* in Bouverie Street, and at *The Times* and *Sunday Times* in Gray's Inn Road. It was only at that point that the workers in Gray's Inn Road realised fully that they too were being threatened.

The unions asked for assurances that existing terms and conditions would be protected for all staff including any workers moving to Wapping - an elementary part of any relocation terms to protect jobs and conditions. This was derided and swept aside by the company and paraded subsequently by the management as if the trade unions were seeking 'jobs for life' for their members.

Every attempt to open a discussion and negotiation was blocked and repelled by the management. Finally, when the company decided unilaterally to give notice to scrap all union agreements across the four national newspapers, the unions decided to declare a dispute and conduct a ballot for industrial action including a strike.

The workers voted by a huge margin to strike in defence of their conditions of employment and the strike began on the evening of Friday 24 January 1986, less than a year after the end of the miners' strike. Letters giving notice of dismissal were given out to people as they left the buildings. That night and during the weekend Murdoch's management team began production of the newspapers at Wapping using the secretly recruited and EETPU-organised workforce and with the editorial and managerial staffs that had agreed to accept a £2000 bribe to transfer on management terms. A second letter of dismissal was sent out on 27 January.

Five thousand five hundred men and women from all grades and categories of workers were sacked, never to be reinstated: production workers and printers, clerical and warehouse staffs, cleaners and canteen workers, and some journalists who were appalled at the company's actions and refused to transfer to Wapping under new terms. Four trade unions – SOGAT (Society of Graphical and Allied Trades), the NGA, the AUEW (Amalgamated Union of Engineering Workers (AUEW) and the NUJ - joined forces for the duration of the dispute.

As the dispute progressed through 1986, all the reports of the recruitment of a scab workforce that the management had denied were proven to be true. Within a couple of weeks of the strike beginning a letter leaked from the company's lawyers, Farrer's, was published by the *Morning Star.* It revealed that the advice given to the company months before was how to secure a watertight pretext for sacking the workforce, and further how to ensure that the greatest number would be caught, by dismissing them at the beginning of a weekend. (4)

Within less than a week the company had secured court orders instructing the print unions not to order members to take solidarity action, and ordering other unions not to issue instructions to members to observe picket lines and requests for solidarity. Even local authorities later on in 1986 were a subject of court orders preventing them from boycotting News International titles in libraries.

SOGAT (the larger of the two print unions) was fined and had its funds and assets seized by the courts during its four-month long instruction to newspaper wholesale workers not to handle the Murdoch titles. The NGA was also fined, but managed to avoid sequestration.

News International returned to court in the summer of 1986 to try to stop the demonstrations and picketing at Wapping and at the TNT distribution depots. Some new restrictions were applied by the court, but the demonstrations and picketing continued. (5) However, early in 1987, after the sacked workers had twice rejected offers which provided compensation but no jobs and no trade union recognition, the company threatened to go back to court. Fearing that News International would be successful in any new court action, first SOGAT and then the NGA decided to end the dispute. Although in some sections a number of the sacked workers had left the struggle, the majority had remained loyal to each other and were furious and bitter at the outcome. Compensation which had been rejected some months before was paid and the demonstrations and picketing ended. No-one was reinstated and the unions remain unrecognised by the company.

Throughout the dispute, there were fearful scenes of police violence but, as with the miners, it was all blamed on printworkers and their supporters. BBC and ITV film crews had also been attacked by the police, and MPs who were present on several occasions when police ran riot through peaceful marchers and demonstrators made calls in the House of Commons for public enquiries.

The policing of the miners' and the printworkers' struggles have formed the model for policing of disputes and protest ever since. Under the pretext of maintaining public order but behaving as a militia or a private army, the police acted to ensure that the employer was able to continue their business and trade and prevent the workers from forming an effective picket. The trade unions ended up in court and fined heavily, the workers in hospital casualty departments or gaol and bound over or fined. (6)

The so-called 'Farrer's letter' exposed the tactics to provoke a dispute and justify dismissal of an entire workforce, and the documents presented in court actions by the company demonstrated conclusively that shadow companies had been created during the first half of 1985 to ensure that any action by the trade unions would be illegal. Even though the company had sacked them and moved their workplace to Wapping, the only places that were legal to picket were the empty buildings of their original employers.

Through the emerging scandal of phone-hacking and corrupt relationships with police and politicians many, possibly most, people would believe that Murdoch and his team are capable of anything. In 1986 printworkers and the journalists who supported them - the "refuseniks" - knew that all along, yet when they tried to explain to people what the company had done it sounded like a fantasy. Murdoch was able to use the anti-union laws newly-minted during the 1980s, but still in full operation 30 years later, to block trade union solidarity action and to render workers' efforts to protect themselves and each other ineffective. The removal of effective trade union organisation had serious implications for press ownership and freedom too.

The other newspaper employers took their cue from Murdoch (7) : Robert Maxwell at the *Daily Mirror*, United Newspapers at the Express group, *Daily Mail* owners Associated Newspapers, *The Guardian*, the *Financial Times* and later the Telegraph group made thousands of workers redundant during their moves to new production and publishing sites in London's former docklands. All the proprietors sought substantial changes in terms and conditions, and some derecognised the print unions and the NUJ during the period of demoralisation post-Wapping. Irrespective of whether the unions had already agreed and accepted "new technology", the myths of universal printworker resistance to change and responsibility for every conceivable kind of bad employment practice became the accepted explanation for the ills of Fleet Street. Commentators and academics took up and repeated the lie that

Fleet Street workers had brought it all upon themselves and that Murdoch's dash for freedom (from the unions) enabled the newspaper industry to become profitable by embracing new technology and reducing jobs. It was claimed fewer jobs and costs would mean a more diverse press and greater press freedom.

In 1986, eight companies or individuals controlled the 17 national daily and Sunday newspapers (8). Three of those companies accounted for 78% of newspaper sales. Several national newspapers were launched in the aftermath of Wapping, only *The Independent* survived. Shah sold Today to Lonrho. It then passed to Murdoch's News International and was closed in 1994. The only other national newspaper launch some years later was the soft-porn *Daily Star.*

Today, with fewer national newspapers not more and with another major closure by Murdoch with the demise of the *News of the World*, three companies control 70% of daily national newspaper circulation; the five largest regional newspaper publishers control 70% of circulation; the top five newspaper owners account for more than 70% of traffic to the top 50 news websites. (9)

And what of workers' jobs and trade union rights and freedoms? Screaming headlines in the national and local press created the atmosphere of hatred for state-owned utilities and industries; public services industries were badly run and should be privatised; local authorities with their statutory duties to provide housing were starved of funding and ordered to sell precious housing stock on demand. Civil rights relating to dissent, and defence of jobs and conditions were restricted to render workers powerless to take effective action to protect themselves both at work and in the community. The ability of trade unions to organise and mobilise workers by strike action, by solidarity or sympathy action, or by picketing, shrank, and local councils and councillors were penalised for protecting their communities.

The febrile atmosphere of the eighties ensured that trade unionists and workers in general were held to be responsible for both the problems within their own industries and workplaces and the chaos, deprivation and poverty which were to follow privatisation and unemployment.

A constant barrage of anti-union propaganda presented as news in the press, tv and radio ensured that, after Wapping and the melt-down in Fleet Street, there was no impediment to democratic organisations and elected representatives being pilloried to the point of destruction. Stories of conspiracy were freely invented and presented as fact such as in the case of the NUM and Arthur Scargill.

Well-paid, well-organised print workers had always been the subject of criticism by their employers in the columns of the newspapers they produced. When that criticism lapsed further into abuse or falsehood about themselves or other workers such as the Grunwick workers, health workers (10) or miners, printworkers had the ability, although not the right, to lodge a protest or take action to insist on the right of reply if the newspaper proprietor refused to take out the offending article. When proprietors failed to respond, printworkers had the choice, not the right, to take action or not.

Newspaper editors and proprietors claimed infringement of editorial freedom every time Fleet Street workers took a principled stand in this way and were as vitriolic and united in their condemnation as they have been resisting any efforts to apply fairer standards of reporting and behaviour arising from the Leveson inquiry and the phone-hacking scandal.

News International remains the only company that refuses to recognise the print and media unions in any of their divisions. But the weakened state of trade union organisation in national newspapers since the Wapping dispute together with the anti-union laws has meant that no action has been able to be taken in almost 30 years to apply the right of reply. Print and media workers have no protection from unprincipled management instruction or coercion. The consequences are there for all to see: far from a free press, the proprietors have simply created a right to say and do what they please under the guise of the freedom of the press.

Newspapers, book and magazines have always been recognised as having a particular importance for information and education and therefore being of political and social importance. Means of communicating ideas have serious implications for democracy and basic rights and the ability of every person to act as a free citizen, hence VAT zero-rating and the newspaper rate for postage.

With the press and media dominated by three or four corporations, restoration of union rights for all grades of worker supported by a conscience clause to empower journalists to refuse instructions to work unethically without putting their jobs at risk, is as important for press freedom and diversity as the need for ownership caps within and across the sectors of the industry.

Notes:

1) Roy Greenslade, *Press Gang: How newspapers make profits from propaganda*, Pan Books, 2004.

2) Linda Melvern, *The End of the Street*, Methuen, 1986.

3) For reports and a selection of documents 1980-86 see News International Dispute Archive: *http://www.wapping-dispute.org.uk/origins-pt1-documents; and http://www.wapping-dispute.org.uk/origins-pt2-documents;*

4) SOGAT Strike Bulletin: *http://www.wapping-dispute.org.uk/sites/default/files/4-1986-sogat-strike-bulletin-1--feb-.pdf*; *Morning Star*, 4th February 1986 (Peoples Press Printing Society) and see *http://www.wapping-dispute.org.uk/anti-union-laws-documents*

5) *Print*: journal of the National Graphical Association, September 1986: *http://www.wapping-dispute.org.uk/sites/default/files/_mg_7439--298-of-1411-.pdf*

6) For details of police activity see *Hansard* , 8 May 1986; 25 July 1986; 26 January 1987; other reports: *http://www.wapping-dispute.org.uk/support-the-company* ; and *http://www.wapping-dispute.org.uk/brutality*

7) *Labour Research*, March 1986: *http://www.wapping-dispute.org.uk/sites/default/files/lrd-1986-mar-sacking-threats-spread.pdf*; Wapping Post, August 1986: *http://www.wapping-dispute.org.uk/sites/default/files/last-exit-to-wapping.pdf*

8) *Labour Research*, March 1986: *http://www.wapping-dispute.org.uk/sites/default/files/4-w7-story-fleet-street-the-companies-mar-1986-lrd-article-who-controls-the-media.pdf* ; and February 1990: *http://www.wapping-dispute.org.uk/sites/default/files/lrd-1990-feb-media-moguls-cross-media-ownership.pdf*;

9) *Free Press* (CPBF, no 198, March-April 2014, p8) and *www.cpbf.org.uk*; Media Reform: *http://www.mediareform.org.uk/wp-content/uploads/2013/05/Submission-to-Lords-Select-Committee-on-Communications-May-2013.pdf*

10) Right of Reply *http://www.wapping-dispute.org.uk/unions-part1-images*

Life on the nationals
Paul Routledge

As the late Max Bygraves used to say, "Let me tell you a story." This one, if not true then it should have been. Ron Mount, crime reporter of the *News of the World* in the 1960s, was built like a copper, and dressed like one, trilby, belted mackintosh and all. Sent to interview an erring vicar in a Sussex village, he knocked on the door of the parsonage and announced his intentions. "How do I know you're from the *News of the World*?" whimpered the cleric. "Well," replied Ron, deeply hurt at this aspersion to his professional credentials, "I've admitted it, haven't I?"

The rest of the anecdote was always lost in loud laughter in the bar, so I never knew the fate of the poor man of the cloth. The point was that Ron felt a keen sense of belonging to his newspaper. He was Mount of the Screws. In those days, we were always of the paper and we talked about 'my' paper, until Rupert Murdoch punctured this pleasing myth with his snarl of 'It's my newspaper'. It was never 'our' newspaper, of course, but proprietors were happy to let us think it so, and even encouraged a certain esprit de corps amongst the journalists.

In a career – correction, fitful continuous employment – spanning nearly 50 years, I've worked for pretty well every kind of newspaper owner from the absentee landlord through the well-meaning but unbusinesslike trust to Moloch (perhaps that should read 'Murdoch') himself. Most of the time you don't think about the proprietor, much less the propriety of his ownership. You get on with the job. There is always more to write, more deadlines to meet and more socialising in the pub to bother with than worrying about the remote hand of the ultimate bosses. The Editor was quite superior enough to be getting on with.

So when I went to the *Northern Despatch*, the evening paper in Darlington, after leaving Nottingham University in the summer of 1965, I knew the title was owned by Westminster Press, because I'd been hired by the group after an interview in London. That was practically all I knew (or cared) about the group, except that it also owned the *Oxford Mail*, where I would far rather have been despatched. I was a beneficiary of Westminster Press' policy of shifting graduate trainees around, moving to the *Evening Argus* in Brighton in 1966.

There, I was more concerned with avoiding an editor, Victor Gorringe, who didn't want me, than with the ultimate employer. I heaved a sigh of relief when he made no objection to my breaking my indentures to join the *Manchester Evening News* as industrial correspondent in their London office on 1 January 1968. Fleet Street! And it really was in 'the street of broken dreams', above the Post Office in premises hitherto also occupied by *The Guardian*, opposite the *Dundee Courier* and the *Yorkshire Post*. Down the Street were *The Scotsman*, the *Glasgow Herald*, the *Telegraph*, the *Express*, the *Liverpool Daily Post*, the pubs, the greasy spoon cafes and a village of fellow hacks.

Heaven! We talked about the union – virtually everyone was a member, and 'house agreements' had just come into vogue – but rarely about the owners. Milords Rothermere and Beaverbrook may have paid the wages, and we read about them in *Private Eye*, but they rarely impinged directly on our lives. Not until the independent TV companies began eating into newspaper profits, and a new breed of proprietor began to emerge, starting with the Thomson family.

By that time I was on *The Times*, starting there as a labour correspondent in 1969 after brief stints in the London offices of the *Glasgow Herald* and the *Sheffield Morning Telegraph*. 'You don't work here for the money,' I was told. They were right. At £2,200 a year, it was only £2 a week better than the provincial press, and an active NUJ Chapel at the *Times* Newspapers, then still in Blackfriars, opened my eyes to the proprietor question.

Suddenly, the owner wasn't a distant Canadian entrepreneur, but the man who decided whether I could afford to buy a house, and whose battles with the print unions affected me, too. I was working for a world-famous newspaper, the top people's title that made top of the market losses.

Ahead was a long, lumbering conflict, with many interruptions to publication, that only came to a head a decade later. Murdoch was by then in situ at the *News of the World* and his soaraway *Sun*, but it was *Times* Newspapers Ltd, now under the direction of Lord Thomson junior, who fired the big salvo that began the war. His lockout of the printworkers, and everybody else but the journalists, lasted a year from November 1978, and cost £40 million, a gigantic sum in those days.

What's more, it failed. The printers went back on the same terms as before, with the issue of 'direct input' technology new to the UK but commonplace in North America, on the back burner. It didn't stay there long. Newspaper managements across the Street began plans for new technology, and gave discreet backing to Eddie Shah's pioneering battles with the National Graphical Association in Warrington, Lancs. His success emboldened other proprietors, and also woke up trade unionists wider than the printworkers to the future they and the nation's media faced.

The Campaign for Press and Broadcasting Freedom (CPBF) was born about this time. I remember speaking at a TUC fringe meeting in the Winter Gardens, Blackpool, in the late 1970s, with Bill Keys of print union SOGAT and Tony Benn on the platform, and my deputy editor on *The Times*, Louis Heren, sitting in the front row of the audience with a Lyndon Johnson-style scowl on his face.

Ownership, employment, workers' rights, press freedom had become inextricably, publicly and irrevocably entwined. Who did what with us and their papers was box office. We didn't just report the news, we were the news. That wasn't why I went into journalism. It was most disconcerting, but it was to get worse, much worse.

When Murdoch offered to buy *The Times* and the *Sunday Times* in 1981, we were back in the headlines. An ad hoc 'workers' co-operative', Journalists on the Times (JOTT), was formed to make a rival bid. I never had any faith in this bourgeois construct, and declined to take part, chiefly on the grounds that as Father of the Chapel of the NUJ at the paper, I would have to negotiate with the new proprietor and I could hardly negotiate with myself. Hard enough to do it with the bosses.

William Rees-Mogg, our editor, backed the Murdoch bid rather than his journalists and then promptly jumped ship. Harry Evans, editor of the *Sunday Times*, came across to run the paper. Speaking charitably, he was useless. Circulation dived and he was replaced, first by Charles Douglas-Home, nephew of the former Tory Prime Minister.

'CDH' was as Right-wing as they come. The 1984-85 miners' strike broke out on his watch, and he sided totally with Thatcher. He even hired David Hart, a property developer who was funding the scab miners, to write Op-Ed features extolling the return-to-work campaign. He was by-lined as a 'freelance journalist' and when I protested that this was like calling Thatcher a housewife – true, but nothing like the whole truth – I was told to mind my own business.

Douglas-Home died in office, but not before ousting me as Labour Editor at the end of the miners' strike and sending me off to Singapore as South East Asia Correspondent. This was the paper's equivalent of a power station in Siberia, remote but at least warm. I was happy there for nine months until the Murdoch move to Wapping, of which I knew nothing. In fact, I was in the Philippines capital Manila covering the downfall of corrupt President Ferdinand Marcos when the bomb dropped. A telex message telling me to file to new numbers failed to get through, but I was told on the phone by the Foreign News Editor that if I didn't do as I was told I would be sacked.

Suspended without pay, as it turned out. The sack came later. 25 January 1986 was a turning point. I said 'No' to Murdoch's blackmail (and bribery; we were all offered a £2,000 pay rise and free Bupa if we went into Wapping), and came out on strike with about a dozen Times colleagues in support of the printers. A new editor, Charles Wilson, nicknamed Gorbals for his pugilistic Glasgow manner, said I would 'only be crossing the picket line electronically' but fired me along with the rest in May 1986.

So, this is the reality of employment with the world's most successful newspaper owner! The man who beat Robert Maxwell to buy the *News of the World*, who turned the old broadsheet *Sun* into a cash-cow tabloid. That's business reality. Work reality is a P45 with the sum 'Nil' where your annual earnings should be. I still have it somewhere. But in Fleet Street tradition, I took it round the pubs and wet it thoroughly, before bumping into various Observer scribes in the Cockpit pub in Blackfriars.

The paper's new News Editor, Angela Gordon, a Scots beauty who had just left The Times, offered me daily shifts. Within a month, I was on the staff, within two years Chief Reporter covering the likes of Lockerbie and Piper Alpha disasters, and the News Editor and finally Political Correspondent based in Westminster, at the age of 49.

When I arrived at *The Observer* in Blackfriars, it was owned by Atlantic Richfield, an American oil company with deep pockets, which had been persuaded to take on the Sunday broadsheet. It had briefly boosted circulation, when decent people boycotted *The Sunday Times* during the Wapping dispute, but it soon lurched back into losses. Not that this worried me particularly. I'd had enough of involvement with proprietors. The further away, and the more uninquisitive the better, as far as I was concerned. Just send money marked 'Observer' and let's get on with the job.

But it's never like that. Ownership passed to Tiny Rowland, the dodgy German-born entrepreneur. I couldn't fathom why he should want it, except to further his business interests in Africa, where *The Observer* was much respected for its support for the emerging wave of nationalist governments. The penny dropped when it became clear that Tiny was also keen to pursue his vendetta against Harrod's owner Mohammed Fayed, even to the extent of publishing an unprecedented mid-week edition with the contents of a secret Board of Trade report into the Egyptian billionaire's financial affairs.

Copies had to be swiftly withdrawn on pain of legal action by the government, but the story was out. I was at an NUJ conference in Glasgow at the time, and my motion in support of publication was roundly rejected. Interestingly, bootleg copies of the paper I had asked to be sent to Scotland became prize acquisitions, not least among my critics.

After *The Observer*'s move to palatial new offices in Battersea, under the shadow of the defunct power station and miles from our Fleet Street habitat, it was clear that even Tiny's pockets were not deep enough. One round of editorial redundancies followed another, a dispiriting experience, and we were up for sale once more. The *Independent* group wanted us, but the journalists didn't want the Indy, because we would have been subsumed into the *Independent on Sunday*. And while the Indy outfit was highly thought of, it too was none too secure financially. So when *The Guardian* saviour came over the hill on a white charger, we backed Peter Preston's management. I went on the radio to welcome the takeover, which meant the title would stand alone, and said I would now be off to the pub, this being a Tuesday when Sunday hacks were in the habit of so doing. Except, this being *The Observer*, it was a wine bar.

This was not a wise move on my part. *The Guardian*, that great progressive institution, that great protagonist for the poor and the downtrodden, decided that I wasn't really wanted on voyage. I could stay on the paper, I was told, if I took a £5,000 pay cut and returned from Westminster to the newsroom as a general reporter.

As Malcolm Muggeridge once remarked, you can always rely on a liberal newspaper to sack you in the fortnight before Christmas.

It was midsummer, in fact, but the principle (or lack of it) remains the same. I was 50 years old, with nothing in sight but the dole, but I thought 'what the hell' and took voluntary redundancy rather that the demotion. Three heart-stopping months later, I was hired by Ian

Jack, editor of the *Independent on Sunday*, as his political correspondent. The job offer came through by fax and I held it up to ragged cheers in *The Observer* newsroom before walking out the next day.

It was still Fleet Street in the mid 1990s, in mind-set if not in production geography. You could still walk out of one job into another. Trouble is, the ice floes in the river were getting smaller and the distance between them greater. So I stayed with the 'Sindy' for the next six years, working at Westminster during the week and in City Road on Saturdays. And then the Indy titles were bought by Mirror Group Newspapers, and we moved lock stock and smoking expenses sheets to the 22nd floor of Canary Wharf in Docklands.

Apart from the spectral appearances of chief executive David Montgomery in the newsroom every Saturday afternoon (when I always seemed to have my feet on the desk and could never decide whether to take them off in his presence, so didn't) nothing very much changed. The paper was still very independent of the Major government, indeed, largely pro-Labour, which suited me, though not the leadership of Tony Blair. With the advent of a Labour government, and many MPs and ministers I had known for years, I was as happy as Larry. Well, as happy as my friend Larry Whitty had been before Blair sacked him as general secretary of the Labour Party.

Alas, the redundancy train was forever drawing into the Indy station, and I only succeeded in hopping off with ultimate guile (and the backing of editor Peter Wilby) before the final call to another place came out of the blue in late May 1998. Piers Morgan (for it was he) rang me up to come and have a chat. I didn't know him, or much about him, but I met him in a wine bar in Canary Wharf and he offered me the job of Chief Political Commentator of *The Mirror* (as it then was, he later went back to the old title of *Daily Mirror*).

My flabber had never been more gasted. The salary was scary, the responsibilities huge. I didn't hesitate. I resigned the next day, and started on 1 June. Thus started the roller-coaster of the Piers years, followed by the less crazy but still lively years of Richard Wallace. While on the heavies, I always used to say that inside every broadsheet man there's a tabloid hack struggling to get out, and vice-versa. We're all just scribblers, really. And I'm still there, after nearly 15 years, chiefly as a columnist, though I do get sent on the weirdest jobs, like challenging a ban on flat caps in a pub in Chorley, Lancs. Loadsafun, that.

Looking back on that rackety half-century in the game, let's not call it a profession, it isn't, what lessons have I learned about newspapers and their owners? One, there is no such thing as a beneficent private proprietor. They are all either mad, or possessed of such monstrous self-belief as makes no difference. Two, you can't trust any of them to put their faith in journalism. Three, they will sack you as soon as look at you, with no rhyme or reason. Four, they all have far too much money, which corrupts them and dictates their political outlook.

In my experience, it is better to be employed by a publicly-quoted, soundly-managed newspaper company rather than a rich magnate or self-serving trust like *The Guardian*. At least they observe the niceties of employment law, most of the time. And they are less likely to lay down an editorial line that has staff shaking their heads in disbelief. Contrary to myth, mad, bad proprietors don't spend all day rewriting the copy. They're too busy empire-building. They employ like-minded editors on whom they can rely to set the political direction of the paper. Murdoch is right. They are not 'our' newspapers. We just work there.

The ethos of the workhouse
Martin Shipton

Like most print journalists, I find the idea of being a company loyalist repellent. It's possible, indeed crucial, to be loyal to the paper you work for – but corporate loyalty, if appropriate at all, is the domain of those who work for the commercial departments.

I've been an employee of Trinity Mirror for as long as the group has existed, but only recently, as the demise of Britain's regional newspaper industry has increasingly seemed to become inevitable, have I reluctantly come to define myself as such.

Trinity Mirror came into existence in 1999, three years after Trinity (without the Mirror) had bought most of the titles owned by Thomson Regional Newspapers. I'd joined TRN for the final year of its existence, hired to work in Cardiff for Wales on Sunday. Previously I had worked for another departed giant, *Westminster Press*, at the *Northern Echo* in Darlington. From the time I moved to Cardiff, and in the early Trinity Mirror years, it was possible to get on with your job as a journalist without being unduly aware of your owner's identity. Of course there were academics, and those who took the politics of journalism especially seriously, who worried in public about the dominance of

Trinity Mirror in the regional newspaper industry, seeing it as a threat to media plurality. But at *Wales on Sunday* such concerns seemed purely theoretical and, if the truth be told, irrelevant. I certainly took the view that such a narrative relied on the fallacious presumption that there was a central command issuing edicts that laid down a uniform editorial line, and that deviation from that line would not be tolerated.

My experience at *Wales on Sunday* was exactly the opposite of that. In 1997 I was able to persuade my editor to back the 'Yes' campaign in the run-up to the referendum on establishing a Welsh Assembly. Our morning stablemate, the *Western Mail*, took the same position, but our sister evening paper, the *South Wales Echo*, was in the 'No' camp. After the narrow 'Yes' victory, the attention turned to who would be Labour's leader at the first Assembly election. After Ron Davies' enforced resignation following the infamous Clapham Common incident, we at Wales on Sunday launched an all-out assault against Tony Blair's attempt to impose his preferred candidate, Alun Michael, on the Welsh party, most of whose members backed Rhodri Morgan. We were vigorous in our tactics, carrying a cartoon dominating the front page that depicted Blair with a Pinocchio nose ('Keep Your Nose Out, Mr Blair' was the headline) and printing the phone number of the 10 Downing Street switchboard after some Tammany Hall tactics deprived Morgan of victory (the switchboard was jammed that Sunday morning by angry WoS readers).

The heartening thing was that nobody in the group hierarchy sought to stop us. This was – or so we thought – freedom of the press in manifest action. It certainly was for the small number of us involved in putting the political pages of the paper together – to be precise, the editor and me. We may have been naïve, but no-one could deny us the heady joy of being able to write what we wanted to write without interference from our paymasters. Had we found the perfect proprietor – one who keeps at a distance and allows the journalists they employ to follow their instincts?

In early 2000 the editor and I decided I should stand in a Parliamentary by-election as a 'Wales on Sunday: Match Funding Now' candidate, protesting against the UK Government's refusal to chip in extra money to the aid coming to the poorest parts of Wales from the EU. Such a mixture of journalistic intrepidity and political engagement was truly exhilarating – especially when Alun Michael was forced out of office because of the very same issue days after the by-election. This was surely what being a journalist was all about. If I gave it a moment's thought, I was grateful to *Trinity Mirror* for its corporate inactivity in my direction. If only things hadn't changed.

By 2003 I had followed my editor at *Wales on Sunday* across to the *Western Mail* as chief reporter. I was also by then the National Union of Journalists (NUJ) Father of the Chapel (FoC), our Chapel having around 120 members split between the three papers already mentioned and a series of weeklies based in the South Wales Valleys. The three main papers, like many others across the UK, were in the midst of long-term circulation declines, with occasional rises after a promotional campaign or a relaunch. But circulation loss was largely ignored because of juicy advertising revenues bolstered by bilingual advertisements for public sector jobs and a booming housing market.

Two things happened to spoil our idyll: the group's response to the internet and an initially gratuitous cost-cutting programme aimed at securing unsustainably high profits. Even before what we suspected at the time and now know for sure was the disastrous decision to put the papers' entire news content free online, *Trinity Mirror* had thrown good money away by hiring large numbers of staff to design and create a network of websites carrying soft content like entertainment guides and restaurant listings. I remember an occasion when I visited the Cardiff operation on a floor of an office block round the corner from where our papers were produced. It appeared to be as well staffed as the *Western Mail*'s newsroom and I recall wondering where the revenue was coming from to sustain such a team. It was no surprise when a short time later the great majority of those involved in the project were made redundant and the office block vacated.

When Sly Bailey became chief executive of *Trinity Mirror* in early 2003 she immediately launched a cost-cutting programme aimed at boosting profits. This reflected a firm belief that the way to increase profits was not by increasing turnover, but by downsizing the workforce. Bailey's rare messages to staff at the time emphasised the need for the group to be 'leaner and fitter'. Later that year the first redundancies in Cardiff were announced, commencing a process that had much in common with the never-ending tours of fading rock stars. Trinity Mirror centres across Britain became aware that at irregular intervals they would be hit by a new wave of redundancies. As a result of the consequent savings, profit margins soared. In 2005 our centre recorded a profit on turnover ratio nudging 40% - a far cry from the 1980s, when regional newspaper centres aspired to margins of just 10%. In the main, chapels acceded to the redundancies because there was a plentiful supply of volunteers for the exit door: some were happy to take early retirement with an unexpected lump sum a couple of years before they were due to go anyway, while some younger staff members simply fancied a change. There were still plenty of jobs available in the industry generally, so in that early period of restructuring anxiety hadn't reached an existential level.

At first the impact on the newspapers wasn't that great – and certainly readers would have been hard pushed to notice any change. In the case of the local papers, the staple stories from courts and council continued to be produced. The loss of reporters, feature writers, sub editors and photographers was absorbed with much less pain than would be the case later.

Concerns increased considerably after the second round of editorial redundancies in late 2005, and as a union we decided to alert Welsh politicians about our fears for the future. We commissioned a report from Dr James Thomas of Cardiff University's School of Journalism, asking him to outline his view of the state of the newspaper industry in Wales, particularly focusing on Trinity Mirror's titles. As part of the redundancy consultation, there was a proposal to merge two of the weekly papers in the Valleys. He wrote: "It is crucial that Welsh regional and local papers are given the resources to effectively provide the quality national, regional and local journalism that the Welsh public need and want. And this is not an argument in which public service and commercial self-interest should be seen as in conflict. For the result of such an approach would be better journalism, larger newspaper circulation, a more informed public – and high profits over the long term. Short-term profit maximisation at the expense of investment in journalism will only weaken the long-term future health of the Welsh press.

"The current – and potential – importance of the Welsh regional and local press should not be underestimated. They hold the main key to informing people about issues important to Wales, be they local, regional, national or global. The lack of coverage of Wales in the UK media makes a vibrant Welsh press all the more vital. The evidence clearly suggests that democracy in Wales will inevitably suffer with further cuts to the regional and local press. Democracy can gain – but only if the Welsh press is strengthened not weakened."

Instead of taking the advice of Dr Thomas, Trinity

Mirror followed the path already decided upon by Sly Bailey and her lieutenants. The cuts turned into an annual ritual, but there was an additional twist: virtually the entire news content of the papers was put on souped-up websites for readers to access freely. The NUJ commissioned a further, more detailed report from Professor Bob Franklin and Dr Andy Williams of the Cardiff School of Journalism. Extensive interviews took place with those working on the Cardiff titles. The report, Turning Around the Tanker: Implementing Trinity Mirror's Online Strategy, said: "Employees worry that if all (or even selected high quality) stories are published first on the internet there will be no incentive for readers to buy the *Western Mail* or the *South Wales Echo*. One local NUJ official stated: 'During one of the sessions that Keith Dye the managing director gave recently he said that there wouldn't be any more scoops for the paper, that if we got a scoop it would go immediately onto the web. If it's going on the web what the hell are we going to put in the paper to make people go down to the shop and buy it?'

"His incredulity is echoed in the opinions of many of his colleagues, one of whom commented: 'Why do people want to buy newspapers? They buy newspapers because they want to read something different to what they can get elsewhere. Now if we're going to be putting our best stories on the internet before they get published in the newspaper, then what are we going to get published in the newspaper? If everything you've got is already out there inevitably other news outlets will pick it up, and by the time the paper comes out the following morning things will have moved on.'

"Our NUJ representative continued: 'It just seems to be a crazy strategy that is ill-thought through. What they want to be able to do is to go to advertisers and say we're going to have this super-duper site where all the good stories our reporters come up with will immediately be put up, and that means everybody will want to visit our website so it's worthwhile your advertising on it. But I think that is fanciful, and it will cause untold damage to the papers. You have to ask yourself whether they want to have newspapers in the future.' "

At the same time as the digital strategy was announced, we were told it was no longer sustainable to maintain separate staffs for the papers in Cardiff. In a move that defied logic, the extra work generated by the move to more web journalism was accompanied by further job cuts. Reporters would in future supply copy to all the centre's papers.

The healthy competitive rivalry that had previously existed between the different papers would cease. It quickly became apparent that the change involved a significant amount of story duplication between the titles, simply because there were no longer enough writers to fill the space available otherwise. A reporter would be asked to write a page lead for the *Western Mail*, together with a shorter more Cardiff-centric version for the *South Wales Echo*. In practice the stories are hardly altered, leaving readers who buy both papers feeling cheated. As a consequence, further sales have been lost.

Having to produce more than one version of the same story doesn't just take more time – it kills some of the reporter's creativity and turns them into a process worker. Working for a group of newspapers rather than just one also destroys the natural sense of loyalty a journalist feels towards a distinct title with its own style and character. Without a dedicated team working for it, a paper can easily become more bland.

The next set of cuts hit the weekly series hard. Each Valley's paper was effectively left with just one reporter and without an editor of its own. So-called 'common pages' were introduced, with news and sport shared across areas that had little interest in each other. An increasing amount of emphasis was put on 'user generated content'

– a clumsy term for stories and snippets supplied by members of the public. Inevitably, courts and councils got neglected and the local paper's sacred role of holding the powerful to account was largely lost.

By this time we had gone way beyond cuts aimed at securing unsustainably high profit margins, and were in a battle for survival. The impact of the global economic crisis that began in 2008 combined with the damage done to the industry by itself to push down profits and ratchet up the need for constant change. Trinity Mirror became increasingly dependent on the goodwill of its lenders and had to keep to scheduled repayments of loans – taken out for investment in new technology and to fund acquisitions. The pension fund deficit was also a headache. What confused and outraged the entire workforce was how Sly Bailey's remuneration rose in inverse proportion to the group's performance. By 2011 she was raking in £1.7m – yet under her stewardship *Trinity Mirror*'s market capitalisation had fallen from £1.1bn to £80.2m and its workforce had almost halved.

At the end of January 2013, under its new chief executive Simon Fox, the group announced more than 90 further job cuts in its regional centres as well as plans to focus more on web journalism. Sixteen jobs were to go in Cardiff alone. A bizarre jargon-ridden consultation document was produced for journalists to consume. 'Newsroom 3.0', as the latest digital project was called, involved reporters having to start shifts at 6.30am or even earlier to gather 'breaking news' that could be uploaded to the website in time for the breakfast 'spike' of visitors. The fact that little tends to happen overnight in Wales apart from the occasional car crash or house fire seemed to have escaped those who devised the scheme. Reports from the *Daily Post* in North Wales, where Newsroom 3.0 had been trialled, told of reporters having to file copy to a 'live blog' viewed by few readers, while a diminishing team of writers for the paper had their workload increased to fill empty pages. Meanwhile a new 'shared content unit' was being created in Liverpool to provide all *Trinity Mirror* Regionals with soft feature material like beauty, fashion and entertainment – and another opportunity to cut jobs. Managers in Cardiff sought to provide an upbeat message, suggesting that journalists themselves would be able to devise how the new system would work. But serious doubts remained, both about the practicability of the latest plans and about whether sufficient advertising revenue could be generated from the websites to sustain the remaining workforce and give *Trinity Mirror* the profits it wanted.

Coincidentally, the NUJ ran a stress survey during the period covering the 2013 redundancy announcement. Its results, published at the end of February, provided a bleak insight into how the group's journalists felt about their working conditions. Three of the anonymous comments contained in the report give a flavour of how many Trinity Mirror journalists now perceive their work:

> * Continual 'restructures' at *Trinity Mirror* are putting many colleagues under extreme pressure and stress. It is clear to most that these restructures are untried and untested, and are a huge gamble. Colleagues are unclear on the part they will play and it is extremely damaging to morale. The workplace environment itself is OK, but changes forced on us are considered unfair and unnecessary.
> * Changes to shift patterns, which now include reporters working web-based breaking news shifts from 5.30am and later finishing times (11pm), along with an overall reduction in staffing levels makes it increasingly difficult for me to be able to do my job well as we are so stretched throughout the day. The increase in anti-social hours (this month I will have worked two weeks of 3pm-11pm and one week of

5.30am-1.30pm shifts) also mean it is increasingly difficult to lead a normal life outside of the newsroom. We have also recently started doing two editions of the *Manchester Evening News*, but these changes were announced to us a few days before going live and without any consultation among reporters. It would have been nice to have had some input – it creates a feeling our input is not valued even though we will be the ones with the resulting extra workload. It is simply not possible for the paper to run without people putting in extra hours most days and at a time when pay is being frozen it can become quite demoralising. Talented individuals are being forced to look elsewhere and some have already left without being replaced. My direct line managers (newsdesk) do their best to juggle resources and help reporters where possible. However, worryingly there seems to be a mood among a committed group of journalists that we're fighting a losing battle.

* I have frequently raised concerns to my line managers about operational problems within my own department and in others that affect our department's output. Every time I'm met with the same defeated shrug and response: "It's just the way things are now. Everyone's under pressure." What makes it more frustrating is that management seem resigned to muddle through the day and worry about the long-term issues at a later date – if at all. What personally upsets me, more than anything, is how much we're all expected to compromise the quality of our work in order to get the paper out. It's cheating the reader, for one thing, and it's not what I worked damn hard to get this far to do. The frustration and anger has caused me to break down at work, and I've never been one to run crying to the toilets. It affects my attitude at home as well as my sleeping patterns

– more thanks to the 'rota roulette' we all play, not knowing what shifts we're on more than two weeks in advance, and not getting a full eight hours kip in between lates and earlies. It's a sad state of affairs which I feel can only get worse while these concerns fall on deaf ears, time and again.

Working as a journalist should be a joy, not a chore. The love of language and the ability to find out things that people don't know and reveal them to the world – or at least one's local community – is a great privilege. In its pursuit of big profits, and more recently of survival, Trinity Mirror appeared to have forgotten that creative people thrive best in an atmosphere that enables them to play to their strengths rather than one founded on the ethos of the workhouse.

The group's strategy now consciously focuses on a future where newspapers will no longer exist. Its business plan is built on the prayer that increased traffic to its websites will be matched by increased advertising revenues. Regional centres have been set tough targets to double and triple the number of visitors to the sites. From a reporter's point of view, the worry is that to achieve such targets, techniques that have little to do with journalism are being co-opted into newsrooms. Many people today, it seems, have an appetite for lists of any kind, and are far more likely to visit a website that provides them with 20 random and trivial facts about a person or a subject than to read a considered piece of serious journalism. On the back of such lists, websites are certainly getting extra hits, but whether that will translate into sufficient revenue to sustain stand-alone sites that offer a decent news service once the newspapers have been shut down is very much an open question.

In the meantime, most production journalists have been made redundant and reporters are writing into boxes on templated pages. Once you fill the box, you stop writing or you bust the space which has been allocated to you. For writers used to a degree of flexibility over the length of their stories, a box is a straitjacket that disempowers them. Facts, quotes and elements of narrative that would enhance a reader's understanding have to be left out because filling a predetermined and unalterable space is more important than the story's content.

So the great debate about whether papers should be content-led or production-led has finally been settled in favour of the latter. Which is something of an irony given that hardly any production journalists remain.

Down corporation street: the fall of ITV
Granville Williams

ITV began broadcasting in the London region on 22 September 1955. For its fiftieth anniversary Melvyn Bragg presented five programmes, *The Story of ITV: The People's Channel.* (1) The anniversary was not a happy time for ITV. David Herman observed in *Prospect,* "The collapse of ITV, both in terms of its ratings and creative output, is the biggest story in British television over the past ten years. It haunts *The Story of ITV* but no one addresses it directly." (2)

Melvyn Bragg rightly pointed out that ITV's achievement was unique in world television. No other commercial network had produced so much great television across so many genres. The American networks produced more great comedy and entertainment, but ITV won out in its history series, dramas (single plays and series), long-running children's programmes (*How, Magpie, Rainbow*), and news and current affairs.

But by 2005 those achievements were part of ITV's history. Nothing, in programming terms, was distinctive in ITV's output in 2005 and hadn't been for many years. Also by 2005 eleven of the regional ITV franchises had, for England and Wales, become a single ITV company, with Scottish Television, Channel TV and Ulster TV remaining independent. The distinctive contributions of the ITV franchises, both to their own regions and to the national ITV network, had disappeared.

This chapter explores how a mixture of political ideology, corporate greed and ill-conceived, deregulatory broadcasting policies laid low a great broadcasting structure.

The 1990 Broadcasting Act

'There has got to be a better way' was the view of Lord Thomson, Independent Broadcasting Authority (IBA) Chairman in 1981, of the 1980 ITV franchise process. In their book, *The Franchise Affair,* Asa Briggs and Joanna Spicer analysed the procedures by which the franchises were allocated, and argued "the arbitrariness of the 1980 affair – and the mystique which surrounded it – must go." (3)

However, the next franchise round had a much more devastating impact. Mrs Thatcher's zeal to dismantle the publicly regulated ITV structure resulted in the 1990 Broadcasting Act, which stands out as a malevolent piece of legislation, discredited and disowned as soon as it was operational. Put bluntly, she had it in for both ITV and the BBC which she saw as a cosy, left-leaning duopoly. In a September 1987 broadcasting seminar, with the bosses of the 15 ITV companies in front of her, she had railed at them, "You gentlemen are the last bastion of restrictive practices." She was enraged by Thames TV's *This Week's* current affairs series programme, 'Death on the Rock', and the support of the IBA for it. Andrew Davidson observed, "If the IBA had a chance of influencing the White Paper (on broadcasting) it lost it with the row over 'Death on the Rock'. Privately Thatcher had resolved that the regulator had to go." (4) The publication of the White Paper *Broadcasting in the 1990s: Competition, Choice and Quality* in November 1988 confirmed the worst fears: the replacement of the IBA by a much weaker 'light touch' regulator, the Independent Television Commission (ITC), and the auction of the franchises to the highest bidder. A vigorous lobbying effort by the Campaign for Quality Television, disquiet over the implications for programme quality amongst some Conservative MPs and the appointment of a new IBA chair, George Russell, who publicly aired his disquiet about the 'highest-bid wins proposal', led to the insertion of a quality threshold for franchises into the Broadcasting Bill.

The 1990 Act was still, however, financially deeply de-stabilising, permitting crazy auctions for the ITV franchises but without stipulating minimum bid levels. Central TV and Scottish TV bid £2,000 for their franchises and won them. TVS, the incumbent of the South/South East franchise bid £59.76 million and lost to Meridian which had bid £36.52 million. Thames TV lost the franchise to Michael Green's Carlton TV, a publisher/broadcaster commissioning programmes from independent companies rather than producing its own. Both Yorkshire TV's (£37.7 million) and Tyne Tees' (£15 million) bids were unrealistically extravagant and to cut costs they were allowed to merge in 1992.

ITV had previously sold advertising for C4. Now ITV and C4 would compete for advertising and be pitched against each other competing for ratings and money rather than programmes. The ITC's fatal flaw as a new regulator was that it could admonish ITV franchises but do little to prevent lower standards. For example, the ITC censured Carlton for its 'glib and superficial output' in 1994 and later 'the burgeoning of "infotainment" programmes given over to crime and disasters' but it could not effect change except in extreme circumstances. In 1998 Carlton was fined £2 million for breaching programme codes by showing a faked documentary, 'The Connection', transmitted by the Central TV franchise which it owned.

The disappearing itv regional companies

The Act imposed a moratorium on takeovers until 1 January 1994, but then another period of instability was precipitated. In *The Story of ITV* this is presented by Melvyn Bragg in a positive way: "One thing that had to change was ITV's regional structure. In an international media market the regional ITV companies that made up ITV were small and commercially vulnerable. The major players took the initiative in restructuring. It took ten years, two acts of parliament, hostile takeovers, friendly mergers and huge lawyers' bills but eventually ITV plc replaced almost all of the old patchwork."

This remorseless process of consolidation was also defended in the same programme by Charles Allen, Chief Executive of ITV plc at the time: "Where we are today is an ITV that is on the front foot, an ITV that really is driving the agenda. We couldn't do that with a federal structure. It was virtually impossible to do it. There was (sic) fifteen different agendas and you couldn't make decisions quickly enough. Now we can."

In fact the drive to consolidate the ITV regional franchises into a single ITV for England and Wales was to usher in a disastrous period when, for two decades, ITV lost audiences, advertising revenue and its reputation as a bold innovative broadcaster. If readers want a reminder of what was lost go to *Independent Television in Britain*, Volume V, pp44-48, where there is a long, impressive list of programmes, made by ITV regional companies between 1982-92, which won international and domestic awards.

There was a number of factors behind this success. The Programme Controllers Group was one filter for quality because unsuitable programmes would reflect on the ITV network, but the other was each ITV company's pride in its own programme-making: "That pride was in part related to the desire to associate the company's name with quality in the public mind but more specifically it was to demonstrate to the regulator, the Authority, that not only the word but the spirit of the company's contract was being fulfilled." (5)

One small example of this in action: when Yorkshire Television first won its franchise in 1968 Duncan Dallas was recruited for Yorkshire Television's (YTV) documentary unit in Leeds. The regulator, the IBA, reminded YTV that its remit included making science programmes, and David Dallas was put in charge of fulfilling this. One result was his award-winning documentary *Awakenings* about survivors of the strange sleeping sickness epidemic, but also a popular science series, *Don't Ask Me*, in which Dr Magnus Pyke, the botanist David Bellamy and Dr Miriam Stoppard answered questions put by viewers.

If the 1990 Broadcasting Act was the first powerful disruptive force to undermine ITV, the second was a change in the people who ran the ITV companies. Out went the key figures who believed that broadcasting had a purpose, had to have standards, to educate and inform as well as entertain. In came accountants and financiers – Gerry Robinson and Charles Allen at Granada, Michael Green at Carlton – who saw broadcasting as an economic activity and their first and last interest was the bottom line. Of course these people also reflected the core values of that era – privatisation, deregulation, marketisation and the belief that only a consolidated ITV could survive and compete in the global media market.

Government legislation assisted this fundamental change. In November 1993 the government announced it would relax the rules on ownership of ITV franchises so that companies could own two ITV franchises. In 1994 Carlton took over Central; Granada, in a hostile and hard fought battle, took over LWT; Lord Hollick's MAI, owners of Meridian, took over Anglia. The 1996 Broadcasting Act allowed further consolidation: Carlton bought Westcountry Television in 1996; Granada acquired Yorkshire Tyne-

Tees Television in 1997; and the Scottish Media Group, owners of Scottish Television (STV), acquired Grampian Television. Also in February 1996 there was the strange merger of United News and Media (owners of Express Newspapers and regional newspapers like the *Yorkshire Post*) and MAI. The new company, UNM, purchased HTV.

This consolidation process continued in 2000 when Granada bought UNM (the Express Newspapers arm of UNM was acquired by Richard Desmond). As a result, Granada acquired Anglia, Meridian and HTV, but had to sell the broadcasting arm of HTV to Carlton to comply with the media ownership limits on ITV franchises. In 2001 Granada acquired Border Television.

In October 2002, Carlton and Granada announced an agreed merger. The Communications Act 2003, which received royal assent on 17 July 2003, gave the green light to the merger and the one remaining hurdle was cleared when a Competition Commission report, whilst it expressed some concerns about advertising sales, cleared the merger in its August 2003 report. Finally, in October 2011, ITV acquired Channel TV so that it owned 12 of the 15 ITV franchises. Ulster Television remains independent and STV owns the Scottish and Grampian ITV franchises.

This bare outline of the key changes in ITV media ownership needs fleshing out to shed light on both the processes which led to a single ITV and also the consequences of this. The creation of a single ITV came about through government legislation, but that was itself shaped by Carlton and Granada lobbying intensively for the consolidation of the ITV franchises. The two people who played a role in lobbying before the 1996 Broadcasting Act were David Cameron, the future Conservative Prime Minister, at Carlton, and Chris Hopson at Granada. They had to persuade not only the Department of National Heritage but also the Welsh and Scottish Offices and the ITC that there would be no deleterious effect on ITV's regional output. Plainly consolidation did have an effect on regional output in terms of news, regional programming and the distinctive programmes which the different ITV franchises made for ITV, but the two companies overcame these obstacles.

The same issues arose again around the 2003 Communications Act which allowed the final phase of ITV consolidation. New Labour, in spite of the hard evidence that a single ITV for Wales and England would eliminate what was distinctive and valuable about the regional ITV structure, allowed it to happen. The Communications Act also replaced the 'light touch' ITC with a new regulator, Ofcom, and over the next decade it allowed ITV to abandon many of its previous public service obligations in the regions.

People and profits

> "Our purpose is to serve the shareholder, nothing less. Nothing must be confused with that – things go wrong in business when anything gets in the way of delivering money to the shareholder." Gerry Robinson, March 1992

The other dimension to any explanation for the decline of ITV as a powerful and creative broadcaster is to do with the people who played a prominent role in running the dominant ITV companies like Carlton and Granada.

Michael Green, chair of Carlton Communications, was one of Margaret Thatcher's favourite businessmen and his victory, against all expectations, over Thames Television for the London franchise in 1991 saw his rise to prominence in commercial broadcasting in the 1990s. However, Carlton did not make programmes: it was a publisher-broadcaster with the vast majority of its programmes, apart from regional news, made by independent production companies. Carlton wanted to retain all the rights to the programmes they commissioned from independent producers. This policy led to one independent cutting its links with Carlton. "They wanted too much for too little," said Denise O'Donoghue, managing director of Hat Trick Productions. But in the final battle for control of ITV it was Granada which emerged victorious and here I am indebted to Ray Fitzwalter's excellent book *The Dream That Died* for some of the detail that follows. (6)

Two men played a decisive role in the demolition of Granada's great record of programme making: Gerry Robinson appointed chief executive in October 1991, the same month Granada won its franchise, and Charles Allen, brought in by Gerry Robinson to run Granada Television in September 1992. In 1990, when the turnover of Granada Group was £1.3 billion, the highest paid director received £200,000. In eight-and-a-half years with Granada Gerry Robinson collected £24.2 m and a pension pot of £5.5m. Add to this £3.3 m consultancy money from Compass, £6.3m in shares and a Compass pension of £15m. He also made between £15m and £20 million from the original Compass flotation in the late 1980s. Charles Allen took approximately £30.5m from Granada in the thirteen years and four months he was there – £2.28m a year – and a pension whose transfer value in 2006 was £9.29m. This while freelance programme makers, 80 per cent of whom were graduates, 30 per cent post graduates, were earning well below UK average earnings.

Under Robinson and Green ITV's presence in the regions steadily diminished. Their offices were in London and the regions were leached for revenue whilst commitment to them diminished. The denouement came in 2004 when Charles Allen announced the closure of Central's Nottingham studios, retaining only a residual news base. Regional budgets were cut time and time again beyond legitimate savings. Across a decade Yorkshire Television's regional budgets would decline from £25-30,000 to £4-7,000 per half hour, accompanied by a collapse in the coverage of the region and the quality of its content.

The underlying philosophy of these ITV executives was to demand profits before production, to neglect investment and training, and to divert funds from television into takeovers and ill-thought-out schemes like ONDigital which lost £1bn before its closure.

2006, the year after the ITV 50th anniversary celebrations, was a grim year which saw a new round of closures as ITV folded its news channel, collapsed its Bristol studios, announced the end of children's programmes and cut the lunchtime news by half. Ratings were down 7 percent on 2005 and shares slipped under 100p. Allen resigned in August 2006. Ray Fitzwalter concludes his book: "ITV's traditional role of extending the boundaries of broadcasting and helping to drive up standards was no more. The sadness for some was that replacing programmes and profits with just profits was a disastrous change, instituted some 15 years earlier, the consequences of which were predicted but ignored and then relentlessly fulfilled." (7)

Still not making the Grade

On 28 November 2006 the *Daily Telegraph* cleared its first three pages to run Jeff Randall's exclusive report on Michael Grade's defection from the BBC to become executive chairman of ITV in January 2007. This came just after BSkyB announced on 17 November that it had paid £940m to acquire a 17.9 per cent stake in ITV. It was not the most auspicious news for Grade, who took over in the wake of revelations about fraudulent phone-in competitions, but it got worse as he attempted to revive the fortunes of ITV. ITV was fined £5.7m in May 2007 for 'misleading its audience' over years with viewers wasting millions on worthless premium-rate calls.

One year into the job with the share price at 68.2p and growing concern about the deepening recession hitting ITV's advertising revenue, the honeymoon was over for him as commentators turned cool about his performance. In August 2008 Grade announced plans to cut the £120m regional programme budget by one third, reduce the 17 regional news bulletins to nine, and merge regions such as Borders and Tyne Tees. It was called ITV's Turnaround Plan, aimed at making £35-£40 million of savings by reducing its public service obligations.

In March 2009 the situation was even more desperate with Grade announcing a £2.7bn loss, 600 jobs to go and cuts in the total production budget of £135m over three years. ITV Yorkshire lost 180 jobs at its Leeds studios, which were effectively mothballed, with the ending of *Heartbeat* and *The Royal*, and the quiz show *Countdown* made by ITV for Channel 4 switching to studios in Manchester. The share price fell to 22p.

Grade's response to the crisis was to revert to the way ITV was run under Charles Allen, cutting jobs and programme spend whilst seeking regulatory relief from 'outdated' restraints on ITV's operations. The cuts meant that a workforce of 8,500 at the time of the Carlton-Granada merger was reduced to 4,500. In April 2009 Grade announced his intention to stand down as chief executive. When he had walked into the ITV headquarters on Gray's Inn Road on his first day in the new job staff burst into a spontaneous cheer. Responses to his departure when he finally left the company in September were less demonstrative.

And finally...

In November 2009 Archie Norman became Chairman of ITV and in January 2010 Adam Crozier chief executive. Along with the contribution of Peter Fincham, former BBC 1 Controller, who joined ITV as Director of Television in February 2008, the fortunes of ITV have been partially restored. In 2013 ITV's main network increased its audience share for the first time since 1990. Then it had a

44% audience share; in 2013 it had a 16.2% share of viewing across all its channels and its share price had jumped to 199p. This revival brought in advertisers and audiences for programmes with mass appeal like *Dancing on Ice*, but also by restoring a lost reputation for drama with *Downton Abbey* and *Broadchurch*.

One programme broadcast under the new regime also provided a brief glimpse, and a reminder of a lost vibrant strand of ITV programming: documentaries and current affairs, popular investigative journalism which had an impact. The ITV franchises had Granada's *World In Action*, Thames TV's *This Week*, Yorkshire TV's *First Tuesday* as well as *Weekend World* and *Walden*. They all disappeared in the post-1992 era of deregulated television, but in 2011 a current affairs strand *Exposure* was first commissioned by Peter Fincham. On 3 October 2012 at 23.10 in the evening ITV transmitted *Exposure: The Other Side of Jimmy Savile*. The programme was made for £170,000 by ITV Studios.

When the programme won two RTS awards Maggie Brown noted: "ITV naturally had no idea of the fallout that would then occur, including the toppling of a BBC director general, or the scale of Savile's abuse that would eventually be uncovered by the police investigation prompted by the documentary ... The moral is that investigative journalism does not always have to break the bank, or end in tears. You need committed, resourceful journalists, bravery and great care." She pointed out that the programme signalled that ITV, once the home of *World in Action*, was back in business in current affairs, after two decades of retreat. (8)

It is early days but maybe, just maybe, lessons have been learned at ITV. If you treat commercial broadcasting purely as an economic activity it isn't just the share price that suffers: viewers, advertisers and creative people who want to make distinctive programmes will go elsewhere. However, the ITV which exists today is a pale shadow of a broadcasting structure which, until 1992, served the nations and regions of the UK well. Its demolition was vindictive, foolish and unnecessary and, if nothing else, both politicians and broadcasters should learn the lessons from the debacle, and understand the vital cultural and social role of broadcasting.

93

Notes

(1)   The themes of the programmes were: *The People's Channel, a history of ITV,* 26 June; Drama, 3 July; Business, 10 July; Comedy and Light Entertainment, 17 July; News and Current Affairs, 24 July.

(2)   David Herman, 'Smallscreen', *Prospect*, 23 July 2005.

(3)   Asa Briggs and Joanna Spicer, *The Franchise Affair,* (Hutchinson, 1986) p220.

(4)   Andrew Davidson, *Under The Hammer: The ITV Franchise Battle*, (Heinemann,1992) p16.

(5)   Paul Bonner with Lesley Aston, *Independent Television in Britain*, Volume V: ITV and IBA, 1981-92, *The Old Relationship Changes*, (Macmillan, 1998).

(6)   Ray Fitzwalter, *The Dream That Died: The Rise and fall of ITV,* (Matador, 2008).

(7)   Ibid p260.

(8)   Maggie Brown, 'ITV's Jimmy Savile sex scandal documentary made for just £170,000', *The Guardian*, 26 February 2013.

Power in the digital economy
Des Freedman

Features of the digital media economy

As they are the pioneers of new business models and communicative possibilities, it is time to take the mission statements of the leading social media companies very seriously indeed and to acknowledge the importance of speed, honesty and transparency for the online universe.

First, as Google puts it in its list of "Ten things we know to be true" (Google 2013): 'Fast is better than slow' or, as a new book on digital innovation is titled, it's all about *Velocity*. (1) The significance of speed was borne out towards the end of 2012 when, because of a glitch, information about a disappointing earnings report was accidentally released ahead of time, wiping $24bn (£15bn) off Google's value in just 9 minutes. (*Daily Mail*, 19 October 2012) This was the largest single drop in stock market history.

Second, there should be, according to online coupon company Groupon, 'No BS [bullshit]...We want each Groupon purchase to feel too good to be true'. (2) This commitment to honesty is particularly welcome but hard to deliver in a cut-throat environment as the company found out to its cost when it was forced by US regulators, ahead of its initial public offering (IPO) in 2011, to admit that the way it counted its revenue was not entirely accurate. Following the intervention of the Securities and Exchange Commission, it reduced its stated revenue in 2010 from $713 million to $313 million (*Wall Street Journal*, 24 September 2011), a major embarrassment in the run-up to the IPO. The company has actually had only one profitable quarter since going public and, amidst declining and investor confidence, sacked its founder and CEO in February 2013.

Thirdly, transparency is also crucial. As Facebook has promised in its list of founding principles, "Facebook should publicly make available information about its purpose, plans, policies and operations." (3) This proved to be particularly important in relation to its own IPO in May 2012. If ever there was a case for the triumph of the new digital economy, the day that Facebook went public was supposed to be it. A company which at the time had 900m users (now over one billion), that has reinvented networked sociality, that has unparalleled access to personal data, that boasts of its huge growth potential and that is the epitome of social media dynamism – this amazing company was to be floated and, of course, on the NASDAQ and not on the more traditional New York Stock Exchange. According to the Huffington Post, the IPO was "highly anticipated and was supposed to offer proof that social media is a viable business and more than a passing fad." (5 June 2012)

Yet it proved to be a disaster. Not just because of the technical problems on the day and not simply because the price has fallen so dramatically (falling to half its original price after six months before climbing back up to 75% in recent months). Those are just the headlines. More revealing is the fact that we now know that Facebook's bank, Morgan Stanley, briefed only a minority of investors about its concerns about the IPO, that the company and its underwriters effectively hid reduced growth forecasts from would-be buyers, that the bank set the share price too high with a price-to-earnings ratio of over 50 in contrast to Google's 12 and that the bank was forced to intervene to protect the price, surely far from ideal in what is argued to be a self-correcting free market. (*Wall Street Journal*, 24 May 2012) The deal has since faced a number of official investigations with Morgan Stanley fined $5 million by the financial authorities and with other banks set to follow. (*Financial Times*, 17 December 2012)

This kind of greed, conniving, secrecy and hype sounds suspiciously like a bunch of 'old economy' IPOs and deals in which transparency and good sense were abandoned in the rush for profits. As soon as Facebook founder Mark Zuckerberg insisted on a dual class structure in which operational control of the company by senior executives would be cemented, warning bells should have gone off. (4) Of course, Facebook was far from being the first tech company to do this given that, in Google's IPO in 2004, the executive triumvirate of Sergey Brin, Larry Page and CEO Eric Schmidt controlled 37.6 per cent of the company, leaving new investors, in the words of Page, with 'little ability to influence its strategic decisions through their voting rights'. (5) The great irony was that they got this idea from their 'old media' rivals in the print industry. Page noted in Google's IPO document that the New York Times Company, The Washington Post Company and Dow Jones, all of them the most traditional analogue firms, had similar structures that asserted the right of a handful of executives to retain overall strategic control for the good of the company.

Facebook is now in danger not simply of undermining its own brand reputation but of jeopardising prospects for the wider new media environment by saturating the market for advertising and driving down costs. Media commentator Michael Wolff argues that "Facebook will continue to lower its per-user revenues, which, given its vast inventory, will force the rest of the ad-driven Web to lower its costs." (6) We are already seeing the impact of this on flagging demand for shares in other young internet companies like games developer Zynga (down 60% since its IPO) and Groupon whose shares have declined by 77% since going public. As the *Financial Times* argued (30 May 2012), "There are fears that the turn of sentiment against Facebook has spooked the broader market, particularly investors who previously favoured the sector."

Why on earth would we expect anything else? After all, this is how capital – whether in the shape of the car industry, oil, pharmaceutical or even social media – operates. Yet many influential theorists and commentators have long argued that the digital economy is fundamentally different to the 'Fordist' one that preceded it. They insist that it has not only disrupted the principles and institutions of traditional monopoly capitalism but that the new economy operates on different principles altogether and is able to sort out the glitches, inefficiencies, physical restrictions and information black holes of the old analogue economy.

These speechwriters for the new economy argue that this is designed to be an environment marked not by media concentration but media dispersion where access to niche markets and endless back catalogues will satiate the public's desire for individuality and unlimited choice. Back in 1996 the MIT technologist Nicholas Negroponte predicted that "[w]holly new content will emerge from being digital, as will new players, new economic models, and a likely cottage industry of information and entertainment providers." (7) A decade later, Chris Anderson, editor of *Wired* magazine, the chronicler of the web revolution, now saw fit to highlight the power of the 'long tail'—the almost unlimited provision of niche products that stands in proud contrast to the traditional blockbuster economy—and 'the economics of abundance: what happens when the bottlenecks that stand between supply and demand in our culture start to disappear'. (8)

Indeed, these trends are by no means confined to the media and entertainment sectors alone but are now seen to be forces impacting on the wider economy: lowering transaction costs, stimulating innovation, collapsing barriers between producers and consumers and indeed handing a much more productive and integral role to what were previously seen as rather passive customers. For Jeff Jarvis (2009), Google provides by far the best role model for any company operating in the new digitally-enhanced business era: it has changed 'the fundamental architecture of societies and industries the way steel girders and rails changed how cities and nations were built and how they operated'. (9) For Tapscott and Williams, the online encyclopaedia Wikipedia best encapsulates the possibilities and relationships offered by 'new models of production based on community, collaboration, and self-organization rather than on hierarchy and control'. Whatever their respective conceptual starting points and political objectives, many Web 2.0 commentators coalesce around the notion that web culture is ushering in a far more efficient, creative, smoother, democratic and participatory form of capitalism: 'A new mode of production is in the making'. (10)

The internet has, it is argued, also contributed to a significant shift in the operation and balance of power in society, what you might call (following Brian McNair), the 'chaos paradigm' of power that reflects the dispersed and 'fluid' properties of power in a digital age. According to McNair power:

> ...ebbs and flows between locations and centres, spreading amongst societies along the channels and pathways provided by communication media. Power pools. It evaporates, dilutes and drains away as environmental conditions change. Communication in

the medium through which power resources are disseminated, and leaky channels of communication therefore mean less secure power centres. (11)

Traditional systems of gatekeeping and ideological control have, according to this perspective, largely broken down allowing for more interrogative forms of journalism and a flourishing of perspectives, including even the promotion of radical voices—such as Michael Moore and Naomi Klein—that would previously have been kept to the margins.

Theories of chaos are seen to express more adequately the fractured and decentralised forms of media power facilitated by digital technologies. Jeff Jarvis describes this as a 'power shift' in which "the shift from mass [to niche] is really a shift of power from top to bottom, center to edge, them to us." Chris Anderson makes a similar point about what he sees as an 'inversion of power' from traditional manufacturers and advertisers who are rapidly losing control to newly empowered audiences: "The collective now controls the message." According to Anderson, we are seeing the transformation of power from label to brand, publisher to author, price to free, 'watercooler' moments to dispersed sharing, mass to niche and rigid to elastic while, for Tapscott and Williams in their description of 'Wikinomics', digital 'weapons of mass collaboration' are "ushering us toward a world where knowledge, power, and productive capability will be more dispersed than at any time in our history." (12)

'It's called capitalism' (Eric Schmidt, Google)

There is not enough space in this chapter fully to confront these arguments that power now flows benignly from the periphery and that concentrated ownership is a mere historical memory. There is, however, a growing literature that is committed to proving that, while the internet has certainly facilitated the possibility of the

99

broader circulation of marginal and non-commercial voices, the claims described above are overstated, lack context and are, at times, simply wrong about the transformation of power these writers see as structurally attached to the embedding of digital technologies on daily life. (13) Instead, I want to focus on a few examples that illustrate that corporate power, far from disappearing in recent years, is flourishing and reconstituting itself inside the digital economy. The internet has not led to the abolition of the laws of capitalism but has offered a range of both existing and new organisations the capacity to secure new markets for their goods and services. Capitalism has not dispersed; it has simply found a far more effective way to market dispersion.

The first thing to note is that, despite the rhetoric about unfettered competition and the triumph of the 'long tail', the structure of the digital economy looks a lot like the structure of the analogue economy and is marked by dominant players in all its main sectors. It looks more like a Monopoly board than a boot sale. This is by no means an accident as there is an in-built advantage to those companies that move first especially in a networked environment given that the value of the network increases disproportionately the more people join it. This 'network effect' means that a "single firm can dominate the market if the product becomes more valuable to each user as the number of users rises. Such networks have a natural tendency to grow, and that growth leads to dominance." (14)

The upshot of this is oligopolistic (and sometimes monopolistic) control of key areas of the online economy. Despite Microsoft having invested billions of dollars into its Bing search engine, Google continues to dominate the UK market for search with a 91% share at the end of 2012 as against 4% for Bing. In the area of online video where there are multiple players and platforms, YouTube has a 35% share of the US market and, in the UK, still commands nearly twice as many unique viewers as Amazon and more than three times as many as the BBC, which has also invested heavily in on-demand video. (15) When it comes to digital downloads, the inspiration for Anderson's 'long tail' thesis, there may be millions of songs but Apple's iTunes controls 64% of the market (and even more when it comes to individual tracks). (16) Similarly, online book publishing may be flourishing, but Amazon has a 60% share of the US e-book market and an astonishing 90% in the UK (*Financial Times*, 13 November 2012), positioning itself as a gatekeeper that is far more powerful than any previous single publisher and rather challenges Anderson's notion that the digital economy will see the disappearance of 'bottlenecks' in distribution. In the rapidly growing market for smartphones, a handful of companies dominate the operating systems (just as Microsoft held a monopoly over the operating system for PCs): Google has a 48% share, Apple a 28% share and RIM (makers of the Blackberry) a 14% share. Between them, these three companies control 90% of this crucial market. (17) So, despite the fact that internet technology creates the conditions for a plurality of voices and organisations to flourish, the material ways in which networks operate in a free market economy suggests that Robert McChesney may be correct to reach for imperialism-related metaphors when trying to describe the online world: "The best way to imagine the Internet is as a planet where Google, Facebook, Apple, Amazon, Microsoft, and the ISP cartel members each occupy a continent that represents their monopoly base camp…The goal of each empire is to conquer the world and prevent getting conquered by someone else." (18)

Corporate domination of individual sectors (search, retail, e-publishing, etc) is, therefore, complemented by a growing antagonism as these behemoths seek to ward off future competitors and to protect their revenue streams. Some of the fiercest competition takes place in relation to online advertising markets where the *Financial Times* now speaks of a 'turf war' between companies with very different functions but a common need to 'monetise' their users. So while the largest social media companies have quite distinctive remits, they are nevertheless competing for the same pot of advertising revenue. They are both accomplices in the emerging online world (Google, for example, is expected to pay $1 billion to Apple in 2014 to ensure that it remains the default search engine on Apple devices) and fierce rivals. "As competition grows, a once collaborative energy among the top social networks is fizzling out as they each compete to maintain their own slice of the internet landscape." (*Financial Times*, 15 October 2012) As with any other part of the capitalist economy, competition and insecurity is part of the package. What were once dynamic and flexible start-ups have constantly to look over their shoulders to meet the competition both of powerful rivals and the next generation of energetic innovators as well as to respond to technological challenges, for example, the growing popularity of mobile platforms.

Despite Tapscott and Williams' hopes of a radically new 'mode of production', traditional strategies of accumulation and competition loom large, nowhere more so than with the rather 'old economy' practice of massive acquisitions. Just as it has spent heavily on Bing to challenge Google's domination of search, Microsoft spent $6.3 billion buying up aQuantive in 2007 in order more forcefully to announce its presence in online advertising. Five years later, the company was forced to admit defeat and to write off some $6.2 billion of the business. (*Information Week*, 3 July 2012) There may be a 'cottage industry' at the heart of the digital economy - pioneers and innovators working in their parents' garages and in tiny start-ups - but, as with any other sector of the corporate economy, they are always willing and liable to be bought up by larger companies. Google, for example, has spent over $20 billion on acquiring, at the time of writing, 122 companies, in order to stay abreast of (or, in other words, to exploit) current innovations and to cement its domination of search.

The digital economy, just like the 'analogue' one with which it is intimately connected, is marked by the same tendencies towards concentration and consolidation, towards enclosing and protecting private property - for every open-accesss journal there is increasingly a paywall; for every Creative Commons, there is an Apple which 'tethers' its users to Apple goods and services - and, ultimately, towards boom and slump. (19) The digital economy is far more mature and widespread than it was in 2000-01 when the first dotcom bubble burst, but there remain concerns that many online ventures remain overvalued and locked into a highly volatile search for secure long-term revenue streams. "The crash will come," argues Michael Wolff "[a]nd Facebook - that putative transformer of worlds which, is, in reality, only an ad-driven site - will fall with everybody else." (20)

Whether or not that happens, the more important point is that the 'dynamism' of the online world cannot be insulated from the uncertainties and market imperatives of the world it is alleged to be replacing. Despite utopian promises about the dispersion of new media power, we have seen that the digital media environment is often even more concentrated than its offline counterpart and that highly undemocratic ownership structures are undermining the capacity of the internet to meet the needs of all citizens independent of their purchasing power. Indeed, the clearest example of the extent to which digital companies are beholden to the power of profits above the interests of the public is their determination to pay a minimal amount of taxes. Facebook paid £2.9 million in tax on profits of more than £800m (*Guardian*, 24 December 2012),

103

Amazon paid £1.8 million tax on sales of £207 million (*Guardian*, 3 December 2012), while Microsoft paid no tax at all on revenue of £1.7 billion in the UK. (*Telegraph*, 10 December 2012) The last word, however, goes to Google chief executive Eric Schmidt who, reflecting on why his company channeled over £6 billion of revenue from international subsidiaries into Bermuda in order to halve its tax liability, argued that this was done "based on the incentives that the governments offered us to operate. It's called capitalism. We are proudly capitalistic. I'm not confused about this." (*Telegraph*, 13 December 2012) Neither should we be. Demanding that new media companies pay their taxes in full ought to be just one of the issues on which we campaign in order to democratise new media ownership and to prevent the further enclosure and privatisation of the internet.

Notes

(1)   Google, 'Ten things we know to be true', 2013. Available at: *http://www.google.com/about/company/philosophy/*; A. Ahmed and S. Olander, *Velocity: the seven new laws for a world gone digital,* Random House, 2012.

(2)   Groupon, 'About Us', 2013. Available at: *http://www.groupon.com/about.*

(3) Facebook, 'Facebook Principles', 2013. Available at: *http://www.facebook.com/principles.php.*

(4)   D. Kirkpatrick, *The Facebook Effect*, Virgin Books, 2010, p321

(5)   Google, '2004 Founders' IPO Letter', 2004. Available at: *http://investor.google.com/corporate/2004/ipo-founders-letter.html.*

(6)   M. Wolff, 'The Facebook Fallacy', *Technology Review,* 22 May, 2012. Available at: *http://www.technologyreview.com/news/427972/ the-facebook-fallacy/*.

(7)   N. Negroponte, *Being Digital,* Coronet, 1996, p18.

(8)   C. Anderson, *The Longer Long Tail: How Endless Choice is Creating Unlimited Demand*, Random House Business Books, 2009, p11.

(9)   J. Jarvis, *What Would Google Do?*, Collins Business, 2009, p27.

(10)   D. Tapscott and A. Williams, *Wikinomics: How Mass Collaboration Changes Everything,* Atlantic Books, 2008, p1 & ix.

(11)   B. McNair, *Cultural Chaos,* Routledge, 2006, p 200.

(12)   Jarvis, op.cit, p 11 & 67; Anderson, op.cit, p99; Tapscott & Williams, op.cit, p12.

(13)   D. Freedman, 'Web 2.0 and the Death of the Blockbuster Economy' in J. Curran, N. Fenton and D. Freedman, *Misunderstanding the Internet,* Routledge, 2012; C. Fuchs, *Foundations of Critical Media and Information Studies*, Routledge, 2012; R. McChesney, *Digital Disconnect: How Capitalism is Turning the Internet against Democracy*, New Press, 2013; J. Zittrain, *The Future of the Internet*, Penguin, 2008.

(14)   T. Wu, 'In the Grip of the New Monopolists', *Wall Street Journal,* 13 November, 2010.

(15)   comScore 2013 UK Digital Future in Focus, 2013. Available at: *http://www.comscore.com/Insights/Presentations_and_ Whitepapers/2013/2013_UK_Digital_Future_in_Focus.*

(16)   NPD Group, 'iTunes Continues to Dominate Music Retailing', press release, 18 September 2012. Available at: *https://www.npd.com/ wps/portal/npd/us/news/press-releases/itunes-continues-to-dominate- music-retailing-but-nearly-60-percent-of-itunes-music-buyers-also-use- pandora/*.

(17)   comScore, op.cit.

(18)   McChesney, op.cit, p 137.

(19)   J. Zittrain, *The Future of the Internet,* Penguin, 2008.

(20)   Wolff, op.cit.

The sorry future for global media
Gary Herman

For two decades commentators and academics have been hammering home the message that the digital revolution underpins a growing and irreversible convergence in the form and content of our media. Publishers – particularly in the news business, and particularly in the UK – have embraced the change in a way that broadcasters and film-makers covering similar content have not, or have not yet. 'Web first' and 'digital first' have become watchwords as journalists queue for their redundancy payments and local dailies go weekly or close down completely.

If convergence is driving the crisis, why has it not equally affected other media? The reason is simple – the impact of convergence is not evenly spread. Newspaper publishing has long been the weakest area of the media – the most heavily dependent on advertising, the least global in market terms, the most affected by demographic change, and the most susceptible to its content migrating to digital platforms including computers, tablets and smartphones. For years, publishing in the UK has emphasised consolidation – mergers and acquisitions were designed primarily to support core activities by concentrating ownership, not by extending corporate reach, and the motor was always a desire to cut costs and realise economies of scale. As long ago as 1978, an academic report on media ownership, produced for Unesco, observed that "the causes of concentration are only partially competition with other media.... Much more important is rising costs and the structure of profits in the industry." (1)

In the face of precipitous declines in circulation, getting rid of print and distribution bills seems to be a no-brainer, particularly for those newspaper executives who think of their readers as so many consuming units (and that is an increasingly common mindset). But while cost-cutting may be the long-term motive, current trends in advertising are probably more influential. In 2012 internet advertising gained the highest share of the UK's spending on adverts at 32 per cent – up from 28 per cent in the previous year. According to the Internet Advertising Bureau and Warc – the World Advertising Research Centre – UK advertising spend as a whole grew by 2.3 per cent (2.7 per cent in 2011), while internet advertising – covering applications running on computers, smartphones and tablets – grew by 13.3 per cent (slightly down on the previous year's growth of 16.8 per cent). By contrast, expenditure on print advertising shrank by 6.0 per cent for 'national newsbrands', 10.8 per cent for 'regional newsbrands' and 9.4 per cent for 'magazine brands'. Most tellingly, advertising spend with the online versions of print publications rose in 2012 – by 29.3 per cent for national brands, 1.4 per cent for regional brands and 1.5 per cent for magazines. It currently stands at between 10 and 20 per cent of the shrinking 'brand' totals. Similar figures are common throughout Europe and North America. (2)

These trends have one cause: the success of a single company called Google.

Readers who thought Google was a search engine should think again. Google is an advertising agency, today's version of Mad Men's Sterling Cooper Draper Pryce, and the face of the internet for practically everyone who has ever used it.

Google may have started as the developer of a neat search engine, but it has grown rich on the supply of advertising and marketing services through its AdWords and AdSense products. When Google's executive chairman, Eric Schmidt, protests that his company doesn't use the massive amounts of search data it collects to breach user privacy or for other 'heinous' purposes – as he did in a recent BBC interview – it only takes a little imagination to realise that Google actually does use this data to target ads and that – in theory at least – this means that even anonymised data can tell anyone with access to it an awful lot about individuals. As with Google's tax affairs, Schmidt's attitude to privacy is literalistic to the point of obsession. (3)

Because of Google's apparent success in selling and targeting ads, advertising has become one of the only two reliable ways to make large amounts of money on the internet. In doing so, it has helped suck the lifeblood out of our newspapers because Google's algorithms seem to be at least as effective as newspapers and magazines at getting advertising to the right group of consumers. And it does this at a fraction of the cost to the advertisers. Advertising on the internet is all about 'eyeballs' – the number of people who look at your site. So the most popular websites are the ones that can charge advertisers the most and, ironically, the economy of internet advertising is entirely driven by the volume rather than the quality of the eyeballs. In practice, targeting is only important because it builds aggregate traffic.

The other way to make money on the internet, of course, is to sell stuff in the global market that has grown up around digital media. Typically, this is stuff that doesn't involve significant manufacturing and distribution costs: 'information goods' to use a phrase coined by US economist Hal Varian. Varian defined 'information goods' in 1998 as including anything that could, in principle, be digitised. (4)

For the past decade, Varian has been Google's chief economist, which tells you a lot about the company's strategy. Google uses its advertising revenue to fund expansion in the market for information goods, which in turn allows it to increase its opportunities to sell ads and increase eyeballs. Take Google's approach to the smartphone revolution. Google developed and produces an operating system, called Android, for smartphones and tablet computers. It gives Android away in order to stimulate the growth in apps – small applications that can be accessed from a smartphone or tablet computer. And apps need more advertising to fund them, and more advertising to satisfy consumer lust to know where the nearest Lebanese restaurant is, who's selling the best artisan beer this week, or what's on at the cinema in town. This approach is a modern version of Gillette's strategy of giving away razors to build the market for razor-blades.

Other big sellers of information goods on the internet include Apple and Amazon. Like Google, these companies are increasingly becoming 'content aggregators'. Whatever business they started in, all these companies are visibly growing to resemble each other – at least, outwardly. In particular, as the consumer use of new media focuses increasingly on so-called 'mobile devices' – phones, tablets, e-book readers – so these companies seek to supply content for them. Their market strategy is to 'digitise everything', collect it together in the vast server-farms that we dreamily call 'the cloud', sell it or rent it to us, and rake in the revenues accruing from associated advertising.

Today, Google, Apple and Amazon have climbed the ladder of global media companies and are right at the top. Figures from the 2012 FT500 list of global companies show Apple, Google and Amazon are, respectively, first, third and fourth in the ranking of companies with a significant involvement in the media. Interestingly, none of the top four companies in this list is actually classified as a media company in the FT rankings. Apple appears under 'Technology hardware & equipment', Google under 'Software & computer services' and Amazon under 'General retailers', yet all of them are increasingly known for their activities in the media – whether as publishers, distributors of recorded music or broadcasters of a kind. Apple may be a computer company first, but it makes around three-quarters of its money from supplying mobile devices running the iOS operating system and distributing and selling apps, music, movies and books through its iTunes online 'store'. In the second quarter of 2014, less than one eighth of its revenue came from sales of Mac computers and related software and services.(5).

Today, we increasingly associate content aggregators with media platforms and products. Think iTunes, Kindle, and YouTube – think Apple, Amazon, and Google. Evidently, the share trading business is a little behind the curve, yet its inability to make the intellectual leap that would identify content aggregators as media businesses reflects the fact that, unlike mainstream publishers, broadcasters, film companies or music companies, these media businesses have no interest in the nature of the content they aggregate except insofar as it impinges on their ability to distribute it. They're the bulimics of capitalism – greedily swallowing everything they can in order to vomit it all up again and carry on.

Nevertheless, they do inhabit a competitive world and skirmishes between them keep breaking out. In 2011, Amazon released its Kindle Fire tablet to compete directly with Apple's iPad but at around half the price; then Apple and a handful of big publishers fought Amazon and the US Department of Justice over the way the price of e-books was fixed; and Apple sued Samsung, the major supplier of Android devices, over the design of smartphones, claiming a patent on the clean lines and rounded corners of the iPhone.

Content aggregators compete head-to-head whatever the financial markets say. After all, they're all in the same business. In February 2013, *Forbes* magazine, the house journal of America's rich, reported a rumour that Google was going to start opening stores, just like Apple's. (6) And after Google had licensed several PC manufacturers to produce a Google-branded laptop computer called 'Chrome', Apple's CEO Tim Cook told the 2013 Goldman Sachs Technology and Internet Conference that "because we're not a hardware company, we have other ways to make money and reward shareholders." (7) It may have been news to the delegates that the company that de-signed and sold iMacs, MacBooks, Mac Minis, iPods, iPhones and iPads in such vast quantities was not a hard-ware company – but then we know it's a media business.

In 2012, phones running Google's Android operating system (mostly manufactured by Samsung) sold more than twice as many units worldwide as phones using all the oth-er available operating systems taken together. In May 2013, Google announced the introduction of a music streaming service, eventually called 'Google Play Music All Access', to compete with the likes of Spotify and Pandora and beat Apple to the punch. It is certain that Android will in future bundle a music service along with other apps, just as Apple already bundles iTunes and iBooks with its iPhones and iPads. Amazon is also looking at launching a music stream-ing service, doubtless to be bundled with its Kindle Fire de-vice. More recent entrants into the content aggregator are-na such as Facebook and Twitter are close behind with music streaming and video services.

There is a real possibility, if still somewhat remote, that Amazon, Apple and Google will effectively monopolise publishing, the music business, broadcasting and the movie industry. It is probable that they, or companies very like them, will destroy some of the established mass media players. Ofcom figures show that 40 per cent of the British population already use mobile devices to access the internet, and it is the protean nature of the internet that underlies the growth of content aggregators and their expansion into the business of providing digital media content. Mobile devices will undoubtedly become the dominant platforms for the consumption of media. That is not to say there will be no other formats, but they will probably cater to a minority.

The economics of the digital market favour mass consumption and low (or even zero) prices. Mass markets in general encourage a lowest common denominator approach to product development and sales strategies. Cheap content and advertising cash too often characterise the digital media, and these support the development of a less and less formalised system of media content creation in which consumers and producers are harder and harder to tell apart. Old professional skills such as sub-editing and copy-editing are becoming obsolete. A recent survey of self-publishing, for example, found that only 29% of e-book authors engaged copy editors to check their texts. (8) Auto-pitch software makes a good singing voice unnecessary for a recording artist. Upload an e-book to Amazon's Kindle Direct Publishing site and it will notify you of possible spelling errors and typos.

Digitisation has been accompanied by the fragmentation and de-skilling of many of the processes and jobs traditionally associated with the media. This can be seen in a number of well-documented phenomena, all underpinned by the availability of low-cost digital technology:

- the growth of blogging and citizen journalism
- 'small screen film-making' using cheap video cameras, cheap editing software and 'display channels' such as YouTube and Vimeo

- home music and audio production using cheap sound recording equipment and editing software and the growing number of online music stores and audio distribution networks
- podcasting and other forms of narrowcast audio distribution such as internet radio
- e-book writing and self-publishing
- smartphone app development and publishing.

Much of this is, in the best sense of the word, amateur – a kind of democratisation of the media, delivering the dream of communications for all, long-cherished by the left and by community activists. But to see these developments in that light alone would be a mistake. The growing deregulation of access to the media certainly carries with it dangers from the people who use their new-found freedom to lie, spread rumour, promote hatred or fear, or simply to offend and undermine the moral and ethical standards that support mutuality and the sense of a public good. But no less important is the fact that far from equalising access, in practice deregulation is a mechanism for imposing regulation by the market. When that market is global, the largest and wealthiest companies tend to dominate and are capable of suppressing – or absorbing – all competition.

If small companies or individuals could reliably prosper in a deregulated digital market, we might have something to celebrate. As a rule, they do not. For every high-profile blogger, and for every self-published, self-recorded or self-filmed success, there are millions who never make the grade. And the more people try to win the internet lottery, the greater the volume of meretricious trash that confronts us: a million cat videos, bad spelling, and more 'mummy porn' than you can shake a stick at. Certainly, the media continue to be marked by 'uneven and combined development', in which globalising and localising tendencies co-exist and small-scale productions can flourish in market niches; but commercial success on the internet is driven not by access to technology, but by access to finance. According to the survey of self-publishing mentioned above, for example, the average e-book author earned $10,000 (£6,375) in 2011, while the median income for e-book authors was less than $500. (9) Little money is to be made from these activities individually, but the content aggregators can access a global market, and they can exploit the complex and chaotic international financial system in which they operate to cut their costs, line the pockets of stock-holders and undermine commercial challengers. While most e-book authors in the UK barely earn enough to pass the tax threshold, Amazon UK sells two out of every three e-books in the country through determined price-cutting and vigorous promotion, and pays tax at less than 0.1 per cent of around £3bn turnover a year just because the company's registered office in Europe is a smart townhouse in Luxembourg.

And here's a thing – if you thought you were escaping the clutches of Amazon because you bought your books online at independents like the Book Depository or Abe Books, think again; Amazon owns these companies. Like all successful new media enterprises I can think of, Amazon started as a good idea and grew predominantly through the acquisition of other companies and the provision of services to third parties. Do you buy clothes on-line from Marks & Spencer, Mothercare or Lacoste? Thank Amazon, which runs these websites. You rent films from Love Film? Amazon owns the company. Read Superman, Batman or Green Lantern comics on your e-reader? Amazon owns the digital rights. Use 'the cloud' to store your stuff? Amazon Web Services (AWS) has topped the list of cloud computing providers for the last three years, cutting its prices 19 times since its launch in 2006. The cloud now accounts for more than ten per cent of the company's $48bn annual global revenue, providing services for the likes of Netflix, Pinterest and reddit, among many others.

The point is not that Amazon uses its market-power to push prices down – which it does and can do more effectively than any similar company operating in only one or two countries – but that it uses its market-power to satisfy its own insatiable desire for growth. This is a strategy pioneered by Thomas J. Watson – the man who created and built IBM and famously elevated the pursuit of market share above a concern for immediate profit – but with a difference. While Watson sold machines designed and built by IBM, the new breed of content aggregators actually design and build precious little. Instead, they acquire it – and growth means the acquisition of more and more stuff. This often involves little more than rebadging, re-selling or brokering technology or content created by others. It can be a hit-and-miss affair, especially when the motivation is mixed up with the need to boost share prices, the most critical determinant of corporate success in the economic climate of the last two or three decades.

A recent example is Yahoo!'s purchase of a mobile phone app – Summly, which summarises news reports supplied by press agencies and newspaper publishers – for a reported $30 million. News stories about the purchase were accompanied by pictures of Summly's 17-year-old developer, Nick D'Aloisio, smiling as you would expect as he announced his personal commitment to working with Yahoo! The company had what it wanted – a product with which it could boost its flagging performance in the mobile arena, with the benefit of a strong association with youth and a buy-in to the technology of the Stanford Research Institute, which provided D'Aloisio with the artificial intelligence engine behind his app. The purchase of Summly, in other words, had less to do with product than it had to do with marketing, and the need to refresh Yahoo!'s image in order to satisfy stock-holders.

Then a few days later, Yahoo! bought the social media

and micro-blogging site, Tumblr, for $1.1bn in a further attempt at rebranding itself. This, too, came with the benefit of a dashing young developer, Tumblr's 27-year-old founder, David Karp, and a strong presence on mobile devices. Yahoo! seems unlikely to repeat the mistakes of companies like News Corporation and ITV which lost millions of dollars trying to buy into the internet with MySpace and Friends Reunited, respectively. Yahoo! does not need to buy into the internet. It only needs to revive itself and rebuild investor confidence. Despite poor financial results, Yahoo! remains a major player in the new media world, although without a range of globally desirable consumer products or advertising services. But it has rapidly integrated Summly into other Yahoo! products and will push Tumblr towards ad sales, building on the loyalty of the platform's millions of relatively young users, a third of whom are under 25 compared to Facebook with about 16 per cent under 25 (according to Google's Doubleclick Ad Planner service).

As a matter of fact, Yahoo!'s new CEO, former Google executive Marissa Meyer, has been on something of a buying spree since she arrived at the company late in 2012 – 12 acquisitions in half a year, probably a half of them relevant to the mobile market. Yahoo!'s record of acquisitions has been mixed. The company has bought about 60 companies in 16 years (including GeoCities, Kelkoo, Inktomi, Flickr and del.icio.us). Some of these provided core technology or talent, but many have languished in forgotten corners of the empire. Now Yahoo! may finally have a platform from which to sell stuff, although the outcome will inevitably depend on how well Yahoo! has chosen in making its acquisitions and what exactly it plans to do with them. The first signs are not altogether encouraging.

Of course, the drive to sell more stuff has an unavoidably negative effect on quality – it encourages the adoption of conservative strategies based on popularity and proven demand alone, and the automation, or disaggregation, of business processes elevating mechanistic approaches over the application of intelligence. The integration of Summly with Yahoo!'s news service in the company's newly launched iPhone app – unimaginatively but suggestively titled 'Yahoo' – indicates that these faults persist. As one commentator observed "even with the smartest, leanest 'organic' algorithms in the consumer tech industry, the company still faces a big problem: the sour reputation of Yahoo News, which covers as much celebrity gossip and viral Internet videos as it does hard news of substance." (10)

Despite all the evidence to the contrary, the idea that new technology delivers quality is embedded in the marketing of content aggregators. For example, it is a central part of Amazon's genesis myth – rehearsed in Amazon's own corporate history – that the company's founder, Jeff Bezos, left his job as vice-president of Wall Street investment broker D.E.Shaw in order to invest in the internet. Bezos apparently decided to launch a business selling books "due to the large world-wide demand for literature, the low price points for books, along with the huge number of titles available in print." (11)

This would be depressing if it wasn't so obviously the stuff of myth. You only need to note the telling use of the word 'literature'. In fact, Amazon's famous, and contentious boast, that it was 'the world's largest bookstore' was based on Bezos's strategy of not actually stocking many titles, and the most popular ones at that (Barnes and Noble sued Amazon over its claim; Amazon settled out of court). (12) The more obscure titles on Amazon's list were ordered on demand from publishers or wholesalers. Many listed titles were simply sucked into the database from publishers' catalogues without anyone checking if the books had actually been published, or even existed. I have personal experience of that, when it was drawn to my attention that Amazon was advertising a book that I did not complete and never delivered to the publisher. Only a bookseller with no books can do this.

Amazon's profit ratio – at a little over one per cent – is still tiny compared to the 20-plus per cent of Google or Apple or even to the five to ten per cent of more conventional media companies like Disney, News Corp or Time Warner. Amazon cuts profit to the bone as part of its business strategy. Its market value is accordingly very much higher than its profitability warrants.

But the Amazon myth is a useful reminder that much of the business of the new media giants is now based on smoke and mirrors. (13) In the software trade, they used to talk about 'vapourware' – non-existent products announced in order to boost share prices. An increasing amount of the trade of many new media businesses is in hype, hollow promises and quality-free content. That seems to be the sorry future of a media dominated by global content aggregators.

Notes

(1)   Rita Cruise O'Brien, *Mass Media Ownership: An analytical summary of transnational and national trends,* The Institute of Development Studies, University of Sussex, 1978

(2)   Sources: IAB UK (*http://www.iabuk.net/*) and WARC (*http://www.warc.com*)

(3)   Interviewed on Start the Week, BBC Radio 4, 27 May 2013: *http://www.bbc.co.uk/programmes/b01slvgt*)

(4)   'Let us first seek a general characterization of the ICE [Information, Communication and Entertainment] economy. The basic unit that is transacted is what I call "information goods." I take this to be anything that can be digitized – a book, a movie, a record, a telephone conversation. Note carefully that the definition states anything that can be digitized; I don't require that the information actually be digitized. Analog representations, of information goods, such as video tapes, are common, though they will likely become less so in the future.' Hal R. Varian, *Markets for Information Goods,* University of California, Berkeley, April-October 1998.

(5)   Apple's own figures, see *http://images.apple.com/pr/pdf/1006/704/q2fy14datasum.pdf*

(6)   'Why Google Should Open Retail Stores', Greg Satell, *Forbes*, 18 February 2013, *http://www.forbes.com/sites/gregsatell/2013/02/18/why-google-should-open-retail-stores/*

(7)   *http://www.businessinsider.com/tim-cook-apple-is-not-a-hardware-company-2013-2*

(8)   Dave Cornford & Steven Lewis, *Not a Gold Rush, The Taleist Self-publishing Survey*, Sydney, 2012

(9)   ibid.

(10)   Nick Statt, readwrite.com, April 22, 2013

(11)   'Amazon Company History', *http://www.fundinguniverse.com/company-histories/amazon-com-inc-history/*, cited by Wikipedia

(12)   'Amazon.com', *http://www.referenceforbusiness.com/businesses/A-F/Amazon-com.html*

(13)   Detailed criticisms of Amazon's business strategies can be found in a comprehensive Wikipedia article *http://en.wikipedia.org/wiki/Amazon.com_controversies*

119

Authors' rights (and copyright): the
new battleground
Mike Holderness

> Everyone has the right to the protection of the moral
> and material interests resulting from any scientific,
> literary or artistic production of which he is the
> author. – *The United Nations Declaration on Human
> Rights: Article 27.2*

Digital technology has changed large parts of the question about the ownership and control of media. In the days when mass copying of a book or newspaper involved setting up type and running printing presses, ownership of the presses was crucial. Later, anyone wanting to copy a film needed laboratories and to copy a television station required a transmitter: control still rested largely on rights in physical property.

Now that copying is trivially easy, the law of what is clumsily called 'intellectual property' has moved to centre stage in determining control of the media – or of the notorious 'content'. Confusion is rife over the differences between this and the law of physical property – confusion which is exploited in the interest of those corporations that wish to weaken the control that authors and performers – and their publishers – have over copying of works, so that they can make money by copying them.

Thus battles are increasingly being fought over the ownership and control of the words and pictures that tell the stories that inform citizens so that they have the opportunity to make democratic choices, as well as cultural production more widely. "Intellectual property," Mark Getty, scion of the oil family and owner of the Getty photo archive, said as the 20th century drew to a close, "is the oil of the twenty-first century." (1)

Recent debate about copyright has been dominated, on the surface, by the rhetoric of 'sharing'. But what is this, beyond a teenager's annoyance that they can't have the film clip they want, for free and right now, which they blame on the evil studio moguls' greed?

Behind the scenes, the resulting call to 'modernise' copyright serves the interests of corporations whose business model involves making available extracts of and links to creative works, including news reporting, and selling advertising on the strength of this 'content' produced by others.

The debate has taken place almost entirely around US copyright law. This is hardly surprising, given the predominance of US-based information sources in the early stages of development of the internet. It is important to understanding how these conflicts may play out, to appreciate that there are two separate traditions of laws governing authorship and performance.

The two legal systems worldwide: Authors' rights and copyright

In principle, there are two systems of law in the world that control who may copy creative works. Copyright is a property right and is fully tradeable, just like any commodity. It applies, broadly, in the English-speaking world. 'Authors' Rights' are rights of the individual, and stay with the individual. They apply in the rest of the world – and thus are the international mainstream.

Compare the opening line of the UK's law: "Copyright shall be a property right" (2) with that of the French law on Authors' Rights – droit d'auteur: "L'auteur d'une oeuvre de l'esprit jouit sur cette oeuvre, du seul fait de sa création, d'un droit de propriété incorporelle..." (3)

It is clear that this is a right of the individual: the literal translation "The author of a work of the mind shall enjoy in that work, by the mere fact of its creation, an exclusive incorporeal property right..." does not quite capture the full and barely translatable implications of 'oeuvre de l'esprit'.

Copyright is thus fully commoditised. Publishers and broadcasters can make it a condition of a work being published or broadcast – and of its creators being paid – that authorship is 'assigned'. This has serious implications for the income of authors and performers – which source of constant friction there is not space to deal with in detail here, though below it is argued that the production of high-quality cultural works, including journalism, depends on it being possible for independent authors to make a decent living as professionals dedicated to their crafts and arts.

The Authors' Rights – droit d'auteur – system is, in contrast, fundamentally a right of the individual human. It provides the proper framework for protecting the interests of citizens who make their writings, images and music available to the world, often not knowing whether they will later have any cash value and almost always not realising that there is any risk to their reputation until something goes very badly wrong.

The importance of the rights of identification
and integrity

The Authors' Rights system is founded on:

1) the right of authors and performers to decide when and whether to release their work;

2) the right of authors and performers to be credited as creators; and

3) their right to act against damaging abuse of their work.

These rights are known as the 'moral rights' – a poor translation of the French 'droit moral'. Since 1988 they have also existed in a weak form in UK law. (4) Lobbying by newspaper publishers ensured that they can be 'waived' – that publishers and broadcasters can demand that authors and performers agree that they will not be credited and that they will not object to distortion or mutilation of their work. And because they can demand this, they routinely do. The 'moral rights' exist in US law only for works of visual art in signed and numbered editions of 250 or fewer. (5)

The other side of an author or performer's right to be identified is that they take responsibility for their work. In the case of journalism this is essential to the functioning of democracy; in that of song or dance or film or theatre, to the market.

So when a citizen reads, watches or listens to someone else's work, their rights to be identified and to defend the integrity of their work are that citizen's guarantee that the work is what it says it is: that it is, in fact, by Umberto Eco – or, indeed, Angela Merkel. Except that under US law Patti Smith and Henry Kissinger have no such rights, and you have no guarantee.

When work is digitised and can so easily be altered, who else is to provide this guarantee, other than the person who pointed the camera or the person who wrote the words? The importance of individual creators taking responsibility is particularly acute when they are reporting the news.

The citizen/consumer in our 'information society' must be able to trust – to rely on – the authenticity of the images and information which are being provided. That trust cannot be located in an anonymous corporation – whether it be the BBC or News International – but in the moral and ethical standards of journalists themselves.

For example, in Authors' Rights countries TV news reports individually credit reporters, editors and camera operators. This can only be a good thing for accountability and responsibility. Research would be welcome on the effects on newspaper reporting in the UK newspapers of rewriting stories to suit the proprietor's presumed leanings and publishing them anonymously, or under bylines other than that of the reporter. Do these encourage cynicism and lower editorial standards?

And, lest anyone worry about prima donna creators abusing the right of integrity, note that (almost everywhere) it gives only a right to seek compensation after the fact; and that the requirement in international law is only to provide for action over breaches that pass the rather high bar of being 'contrary to the honour or reputation' of the creator. (6)

The necessity of professional authors – being able to make a living

It is vital to the health of our societies, our cultures and democracies that they include creators who are professionals – who can make a living from their creations themselves, not from a day-job or sponsorship or patronage.

Some over-excited internet enthusiasts appear to believe that there is no need for professionals any more – that in the future every need for reporting and for creativity will be catered for by people working in their spare time. 'Look how wonderful www.wikipedia.org is,' they say... until they find the next bit of malicious or self-interested alteration of the public record...

Journalism in the public interest definitely does not work as a spare-time activity. If there is to be democracy, it depends on citizens having access to independent reporting of the news that shapes our views and our votes. A crucial part of that independent reporting – and a partial corrective to media owners' tendency to behave like aristocratic patrons – is the flourishing of freelance journalists, who make a living by licensing use of their work, and have control over the contexts in which it may be re-used.

Some 'blogs' that writers make available for free are interesting and useful. But it is very, very rare that these 'break' a news story: almost always their value is in commenting on what has been reported by professional journalists. Far too many are, on the other hand, simply vehicles for prejudice, preconception and special interests. These do not serve the need of the electorate to be informed.

To discover how derivative such trumpeted spare-time enterprises are, try posting a Wikipedia entry setting forth your knowledge of any obscure subject that may be dear to your heart. Within hours it will, if noticed at all, be flagged with the demand that it "needs additional citations for verification" (7) – that is, it is not a valid entry unless it references the works of professional researchers and reporters.

Many kinds of art definitely do not mix with having a day job and cannot flourish and develop to the full in artists' spare time. Nor is sponsorship the answer. Aristocratic patronage may have produced some great art – of its time, within its genre. The corporate patronage of our times is more often than not a recipe for mediocrity, whether in office lobby murals or the sponsored novel (Dennis Moore in *USA Today,* for one, described Fay Weldon's product-placement tale *The Bulgari Connection* as 'merely cheesy'). (8)

Under the copyright system, a publisher or broadcaster may change any creator's work without comeback and they may, for example, sell it on for use in advertising, destroying the creator's reputation for independence.

Again, journalism provides particularly sharp examples of the issues here. As Samuel Johnson put it: "No man but a blockhead ever wrote, except for money." The alternative to professional journalism is that all reporting is either by amateurs wishing to make a case... or by paid PR shills.

The print owners' attack – all-rights contracts

Creators frequently need to negotiate with monopolies or with dominant players in highly specialised markets, such as scientific publishers. Individual creators are therefore at an inherent disadvantage when negotiating the terms of the contracts that permit exploitation of their work. In some cases creators face a monopsony: there is effectively only one customer for a type of work, and that customer can dictate price, terms and conditions. Where there is not a monopsony, there is what might be termed an 'oligopsony' – a market with a very restricted number of buyers.

Advice from a lawyer is unaffordable for most creators. For journalists, the value of an individual contract in the UK is frequently £200 or less and some photographers may licence very small reproductions of many images to different publishers, with each contract worth £50 or less: in these circumstances the costs of obtaining legal advice for each contract are clearly not sustainable. While unions and professional associations have sought to address this imbalance by providing advice to their members and seeking to engage in collective bargaining, the situation remains unsatisfactory for the majority of creators.

The issue is not restricted to the impecunious. On 11 March 2013 the Earl of Erroll told the House of Lords: (9)

Someone wanted to publish a book involving some of

my ancestors, and asked whether they could use some material that I had at home. I replied, "Certainly, I would be delighted." Then they said, "We need a release document." They put a contract in front of me that said that they would have total rights to this material throughout the universe, known and unknown, in media not yet developed, incorporated and not incorporated—this, that and the other. The only thing it did not include was parallel universes. The contract said that I would have to defend the copyright whenever and wherever required, at my cost. I was not receiving anything for this; I was simply trying to be kind and helpful to someone who was making a documentary. I asked someone legal about it who said, "Oh, they probably couldn't enforce it because it's an unfair contract," but apparently it is not because unfair contracts do not apply to copyright. I therefore asked whether other people had signed this, and was told, "Oh yes, they've signed them. Don't worry, I'm sure nothing will happen."

It is madness for people to sign these things.

Something will come home to roost.

One result of these unfair contracts is copy-paste journalism: because publishers can seize the right to re-use articles, they do, and the ultimate result is that citizens of a given country get access only to one report of an event.

Then machine translation technology is coming along nicely, which may mean that one report is distributed in many languages to save money. The improvement in software's ability to translate is largely due to the Google Corporation having scanned, without permission and, authors argue, in breach of their rights, over 15 million books. One of the things this does for Google is to give its software examples of human translations of very many phrases to work with.

Of course copy-paste journalism isn't entirely new: news agencies such as Associated Press and the Press Association led the way. Nowadays this is obvious when a web search reveals dozens of regional newspapers running identical stories. But clearly these all-rights contracts are intended to lead to a reduction in diversity of reporting.

Partly, this is the realisation of the economies of scale promised in building large media groups; but the practice of content-swap agreements makes it a more general threat to diversity, where unfair contracts remove the 'impediment' of authors' rights.

128 The details of the lobbying and industrial organisation inspired by the imposition of unfair contracts are explored in some depth by the NUJ's London Freelance Branch (10) and the Creators' Rights Alliance. (11)

Making free with freely-given stuff

There is indeed a potential for a flowering and democratisation of expression in the interwebs. But technological determinism does not apply here, any more than it does anywhere else. The flowering is a technical possibility: the economics and control by selection are separate questions, and the evolution of authors' rights law will influence how they pan out. The battle is now over the operation of a massively expanded field of 'intermediaries' who convey creators' work to the public: as World Intellectual Property Organization Director-General Francis Gurry put it in an address at Queensland University of Technology on 25 February 2011, these should be viewed as 'business associates engaged by' creators. (12)

But the Google/YouTube business model, and less directly that of Facebook and Twitter, is (currently) to scrape up reporting (and other works) that others have researched, written, curated, edited and polished – and make money selling ads alongside these.

This model is fatally flawed. Jaron Lanier invented 'virtual reality' and is also a musician. For years he promoted the fashionable idea that musicians should give up expecting to be paid for copies of their works, and should earn money entirely through performance. (13)

Then, in the past three or four years, Lanier got fed up with playing benefit gigs for musicians who needed operations, as he described it in an interview in London. (14) He wrote *Who Owns the Future* (15) – saying some of the same things this author has been saying for two decades. Having thought hard, he has turned his back on the 'information wants to be free, as in free beer' meme.

Lanier concludes that without regulation, online markets will lead to 'winner-takes-all' outcomes. He considers the likelihood that 3D printing will take off – whether in a decade, or three. When you can download a file that prints out a robot that serves sandwiches, or feeds old people, a very large part of the economy will be mediated by 'works' and 'expression' which are theoretically protected by authors' rights, more than by other intellectual property rights such as patents and not by physical property rights.

If such works are widely 'shared', and if the only cash involved comes from servers selling advertising alongside them, what happens then? "Google might eventually become an Ouroboros, a snake eating its own tail," Jaron warns, if "so much information is 'free', that there is nothing left to advertise on Google that attracts actual money." The businesses model eats itself.

It is true that some people want to create works or performances purely for the pleasure of creation itself, or for the rewards of gift-giving, or because, for academics, giving their work away reaps financial reward through better jobs.

Very few, though, want to give up all links with the fate of their work. But the pitfalls of giving up those links are often not clear until you have fallen in. Giving work away depends on enforceable rights as much as does selling permission to use it.

For example: the Creative Commons provides what is, in theory, a framework for granting others permission to use your work on certain conditions – licences, in other words. But the default licence, what you get if you just click 'OK', frequently gives everyone permission to change your work, for profit. As Andrew Orlowski wrote for *www.theregister.co.uk*:

> Texan Justin Wong, youth counsellor to 16-year-old Alison Chang, took a photo of her. Her uncle Damon uploaded it to the file-sharing site Flickr.com – and Virgin Mobile used it, along with 100 other images posted under Creative Commons licences, in an Australian advertising campaign. Wong sued Creative Commons for, among other things, not educating him about the consequences of clicking 'OK'. (16)

Anyway, the Creative Commons licence is entirely meaningless unless you, the creator, have strong, individual, enforceable rights.

Even a creator who does want to give their work away to the whole world, without restriction, for free – even one who really does understand what this means – needs strong rights to ensure that the work stays 'given away' and is not locked up for profit. This is the whole foundation of the Free Software movement, with its General Public License stating that anyone who wants to use the work must distribute it under the GPL.

Whatever some ill-informed enthusiasts may think, Free Software is not against Authors' Rights: it is a cunning use of Authors' Rights.

These issues, too, do not affect only those creators who want to be professionals. 'Social media' websites are notorious for imposing contracts that grab all rights in works that users upload. Because of these sites, almost every child now in school will be a 'published' or 'broadcast' author or performer before they can vote. Some will go on to be professionals. A few will be famous. And then

Facebook, Pinterest and the rest will be sitting on a windfall of works that they own, if these 'click-wrap' contracts are not regulated.

Google's attack on the law – the siren song of 'fair use'

It is no surprise that the new intermediaries are lobbying furiously – and subtly – to change the law in favour of the business model described above. A large part of this has focused on the beguilingly-titled concept in US law of 'fair use'. In fact, this loosely-defined set of criteria for using a creator's work without permission or payment is a licence only to lawyers, to print money. The American Intellectual Property Law Association estimates that it costs $1 million to take a case through the courts to discover whether a use is 'fair' or not.[17] Google continues to claim that its unauthorised scanning of millions of books, mentioned above, was 'fair use'. When, however, the Authors' Guild and publishers did raise funds to sue, Google found it worthwhile to offer a settlement with a headline cost of $125 million.[18] Professor Lawrence Lessig, a powerful critic of copyright, argues against so-called 'fair use' legislation from another viewpoint:

> When copyright law is meant to regulate Sony and your fifteen-year-old, a system that imagines that a gaggle of lawyers will review every use is criminally inadequate. If the law is going to regulate your kid, it must do so in a way your kid can understand… Fair use could do its work better if Congress followed in part the practice of European copyright systems. Specifically, Congress could specify certain uses that were beyond the scope of copyright law. [19]

In 2013 the well-respected anti-censorship group Article 19 published *The Right to Share: Principles on Freedom of Expression and Copyright in the Digital Age*.[20]

This document asserts that "copyright has been increasingly used to discourage creativity and stifle free expression and the free exchange of information and ideas" – without providing any evidence or even an example. It is clear from the structure of the document that its drafters' most concrete and detailed concern was to protect the new intermediaries – named as internet service providers – from requirements to monitor 'content' for copyright infringement (or other breaches of the law) and to block illegal content, which if done carelessly could indeed impinge on the freedom to receive expression.

But the headline message was clear. It is instructive that at least one of the co-signatory organisations is primarily funded by Google. Other participants in the onslaught of lobbying to weaken authors' rights are libraries that, in the absence of state funding for digital preservation, have signed deals with Google.

There is also of course powerful resistance to attempts to shift authors' rights legislation back toward its original purpose: to encourage (professional) creators to create. The 'freedom of contract' is the rallying cry to ensure that the individuals who create new works are free to be exploited to the maximum. The owners of print media, pleading poverty, have a strong lobbying hand here.

In conclusion

The point of contesting concentration of media ownership is to maintain a diversity of voices reporting the events that inform citizens' political, economic and social choices. The concentration of ownership and control of individual pieces of reporting is as significant an impediment to this goal as is the concentration of ownership of the channels by which they are communicated.

To put the question in journalistic terms: Do you want to live in a world in which Rupert Murdoch – or Sergey Brin and Larry Page – owns the news outright, with the right to change it?

Notes

(1)   Unsigned article, "Blood and Oil", *The Economist* 4 March 2000: *http://www.economist.com/node/288515*

(2)   Copyright Designs and Patents Act 1988: *www.legislation.gov.uk/ukpga/1988/48*

(3)   Code de la propriété intellectuelle *http://www.legifrance.gouv.fr/affichCode.do?cidTexte=LEGITEXT000006069414> accessed 17/04/2014*

(4)   Copyright Designs and Patents Act 1988 Sections 77ff : *http://www.legislation.gov.uk/ukpga/1988/48/part/I/chapter/IV*

(5)   US Code 17: *http://www.copyright.gov/title17/92chap1.html*

(6)   Berne Convention for the Protection of Literary and Artistic Works, Article 6bis: *http://www.wipo.int/treaties/en/text.jsp?file_id=283698*

(7)   See for example: *http://en.wikipedia.org/wiki/Chumbawamba* to check for mention on the incident in which the United Kingdom Independence Party used the band's worst-ever composition at a party conference, in a clear breach of its members 'honour and reputation' and therefore of their moral rights.

(8)   *http://www.usatoday.com/life/books/2001-11-23-bulgari.htm*

(9)   Lords Hansard: 11 March 2013 column 54: *http://www.publications.parliament.uk/pa/ld201213/ldhansrd/text/130311-0002.htm#13031134000556*

(10)   See *www.londonfreelance.org/ar*

(13)   See *www.creatorsrights.org.uk*

(14)   *http://www.frequency.com/video/in-conversation-jaron-lanier-james/83585040/-/5-179533*

(15)   Jaron Lanier, *Who Owns the Future?* London: Allen Lane (2013) *http://www.jaronlanier.com/futurewebresources.html*

(16)   *http://www.theregister.co.uk/2007/09/24/creative_commons_deception/*

(17)   Report of the Economic Survey 201 (2011) New York: American Intellectual Property Law Association, p35; cited in R. Anthony Reese, "Copyright and Trademark Law and Public Interest Lawyering", UC Irvine Law Review Vol. 2:911 p 917: *www.law.uci.edu/lawreview/vol2/no3/reese.pdf*

(18)   Figure from *http://www.authorsguild.org/advocacy/articles/*

133

member-alert-google.html; now redirects to: *http://www.authorsguild.org/ advocacy/125-million-settlement-in-authors-guild-v-google/*

(19)   Lawrence Lessig, *Remix*, New York: Penguin (2008) p 267; *http://remix.lessig.org/*

(20)   *http://www.article19.org/resources.php/resource/3716/en/ the-right-to-share:-principles-on-freedom-of-expression-and-copyright-in-the-digital-age*

Andrew Wiard

> "Intellectual property is the oil of the 21st century.
> Look at the richest men a hundred years ago; they all
> made their money extracting natural resources or
> moving them around. All today's richest men have
> made their money out of intellectual property." Mark
> Getty, in *The Economist*, March 4th 2000

Mark Getty, founder of Getty Images, grandson of oil
magnate John Paul Getty, and the author of these words,
practised what he preached. In little over a decade he
grabbed the lion's share of what is now a world market in
photography. His main rival, Bill Gates's Corbis Images,
bought so much photographic oil it didn't know what to
do with, that it poured thousands of barrels down an old
limestone mine.

Welcome to the other Oil Wars. Even in the years Before Getty the photographic world was already at war over
ownership and control. Those battles however were not
fought between these two titans straddling the globe, but
between the oil producers – that is, the individual photographers who created the oil – and their clients.

Under copyright law, then and now, employees lose their

intellectual property rights in what they create. But under the Copyright Act of 1956 self-employed photographers could also be denied ownership. According to its bizarre terms the copyright owner was defined as the owner of the film at the time the photograph was taken, unlike other authors who were and are automatically the first owners of what they create, by virtue of being the creators. So agencies and employers, in particular national papers, would trap those photographers not directly employed by providing the film at company expense. Those photographers who did not pay for their film thereby lost all their rights. Worse still, and again unlike other authors, photographers working on commission would also lose all rights, to their clients – unless there was an agreement to the contrary. Consequently ownership and control of a very high proportion of UK photography fell into the hands of publishers and proprietors. Faced with such injustice photographers fought back hard and, through the Copyright Designs and Patents Act (CPDA) of 1988, won the most important reforms of the last hundred years. This Act finally made self-employed photographers, like all other self-employed

All 64 Daily Express photographers in 1960. Copyright © Express Newspapers.

creators, the first owners of the intellectual property rights in their work, whether commissioned or not (and regardless of who owned the film!). (1)

This coincided with another dramatic change, at least in the world of national papers. In what seems now a bygone age most of their photographers were still employees. Look at this photo below, taken in 1960, a composite of the Manchester, London and Glasgow teams of photographers working for the *Daily Express*. Over 60 of them. At the time of writing, there are only three left on staff and four on contract. First they came for the photographers – blame the accountants destroying our national papers. Savings came at a price. The freelancers replacing the staffers cost the papers less, but the unintended consequence under the new 1988 Act was that they, not their titles, now owned their own pictures. And so did photographers working throughout magazine and book publishing. They, not their clients, would get the repeat fees, syndication rights, distribute through agencies or run their own libraries. Some of them had already retained ownership through contracts overriding the 1956 Act, as did rock

photographer Paul Slattery:

I was lucky to be around in a golden age of music and got to photograph such bands as The Ramones, The Sex Pistols, Motorhead, U2, Joy Division, The Smiths, The Stone Roses, The Manic Street Preachers and Oasis. I have always held on to my copyright and now 35 years later I have a rock photography archive which I own and have been making money out of for nearly 30 years. This helped me pay off my mortgage, and as I get older will be a valuable source of income, as good as an old age pension quite honestly. Bands of this period were very influential, are still popular, and appear with regularity in the international music press both in hard and online editions. My photographs have appeared in literally thousands of magazines, over 150 books, and almost 50 CD releases. I have had two photography books published *The Smiths, The Early Years* from my 1983 and 1984 sessions and *Oasis, A Year*

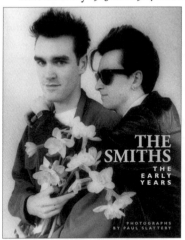

On The Road about the band's rise from pubs to stadiums 1994-1995. I am presently working on my third rock photography book about The Manic Street Preachers. One of my best selling images is this one of Johnny Marr and Morrissey which I shot for *Sounds* magazine in 1983. I have always liked this shot and ended up using it as

Johnny Marr and Morrissey shot for 'Sounds' magazine in 1983, and, as he retained ownership, the cover of his Smiths book in 2007. Copyright © Paul Slattery.

the cover of my Smiths book in 2007. My advice to any young photographer is work your butt off while you are young and motivated, and have the energy and never, never sign away your copyright.

The reforms of the CPDA 1988 made millions, literally millions, for photographers. All this was clearly contrary to the natural order of things. The counter-revolution was not long in coming. For what the Act gave with one hand, it took away with the other – by providing for contractual agreements overriding the photographers' rights as first owner. (2) Panicking at loss of ownership and control, from that day to this publishers have tried to thieve what photographers now indisputably owned through sign-here-or-you'll-never-work-again-rights-grabbing contracts. Take this, one the worst, from none other than Rupert Murdoch:

> *Copyright Assignment.* The Contributor hereby assigns to *The Sunday Times* all present and future copyright in the Material for the full term of copyright, which includes (but is not limited to) the right to use the Material in all their publications' different present and future forms e.g. print, microfilm, Braille, talking book, electronic database, e-paper, website, mobile phone, electronic device or any other facsimile or derivative versions in any medium and the right to include the Material in any book or other publication produced by *The Sunday Times*.

This typical rights-grab speaks for itself, but without going into the intricacies of intellectual copyright law, allow me to explain a couple of key terms. 'Assignment' means surrendering copyright itself, the right to make or authorise the making of copies. As in ownership of a house. 'Assignment' can only be in writing – hence the written contract. Alternatively photographers as copyright owners can issue a 'Licence' to make certain copies. As in letting the rooms in a house, for a day, a week, a month, or many years. Rights-grabbing contracts need not necessarily demand assignment but by extracting licences, excessive all-embracing licences for all kinds of future rights, they can be just as rapacious as Murdoch's, acquiring ownership in practice, if not in name.

Photographers operate in a buyers' market and so are under constant pressure to sign these unfair contracts, fighting countless battles, usually alone. But here's one that photographers won, fighting as a group. In 2001 The Scotsman Group tried to get its freelance photographers to sign a rights-grabbing contract. Drew Farrell, one of those who refused to sign, tells the tale:

> *The Scotsman*'s management announced that, "If you won't sign it then you won't be working for us again "...we informed them that they [must] not use any of our pictures held in their archive. Their reply was a legal one, from a lawyer who struggled to spell copyright (clue: it's not two words, and the second one isn't 'write') and made it clear that Scotsman Publica-

Seven of the eleven victorious photographers outside The Scotsman Building in Edinburgh after they won. L-R: Graham McGirk, Paul Raeburn, Nick McGowan-Lowe, Colin McPherson, Gary Doak, Drew Farrell and Jeremy Sutton-Hibbert. Photo copyright © Drew Farrell.

> tions would continue to use our pictures if required as per their 'understanding'. Backed by the NUJ and its lawyers they took *The Scotsman* to court: Our case was settled on the eve of the Court of Session date in Edinburgh. The Scotsman offered no evidence in their defence nor did they provide any witnesses. In the eyes of their lawyers we had proved a genuine loss. They

paid £100 for unauthorised print use and more importantly agreed to pay £500 pro rata per annum for the use of an image across their websites. Although there was no day in court the action against The Scotsman case is now a lodged public record and as we refused to sign a confidentiality clause we are able to show the outcome. The case involved 133 copyright abuses in the print editions of the newspapers and magazines, and 52 copyright abuses in the online versions of the newspapers amounting to £33,488 including VAT. Of this, £4,794 had already been paid by Scotsman Publications in respect of the print abuses, but this was deemed unacceptable as a settlement by the 11 photographers. The dispute is estimated to have cost Scotsman Publications in excess of £170,000. (3)

Those photographers who managed to fight their battles and win could look forward, like Paul Slattery, to future sales either directly to their clients or through the agencies of their choice.

Enter stage left the internet titans. In 1989, the year the 1988 Act came into force, Microsoft's Bill Gates founded the company that later became Corbis. Corbis began buying up the photographic world, agencies and libraries big and small. Then in 1995 Mark Getty, together with Jonathan Klein, founded what is now Getty Images. A bit late to the party but soon outstripping Gates at the same game – destroying a cottage industry and turning photography into a marketplace dominated by giant conglomerates. An old game, an obvious game, and simple enough game if you've got the money. They both had – in Getty's case he did not make, and did not need to make, a trading profit for nearly a decade. But, know thine enemy – they were also visionaries, internet visionaries. They foresaw the end of prints and transparencies delivered by messenger or in the post. They foresaw the digitising of film and digital delivery over the internet. And they foresaw that after buying up and owning every agency in town, they did not necessarily need to own the copyright in the pictures. Control the pipelines, and you control the oil.

Photographic Davids were now fighting Goliath. No happy ending to this story, as Goliath usually won. While it is important not to romanticise a vanishing world, photographers who had managed to retain control of their work had been able to pick and choose their agents and agencies, and negotiate on terms not too disadvantageous, frequently with agency owners who had themselves been working photographers. Quarrels there were, but quarrels within the family, with agents who still cared – yes actually cared – about photography. As Gates and Getty squared off across the world chessboard, photographers now became their expendable pawns, as most had nowhere else to turn. The titans became dictators. Getty cut their share of sales from 50, the industry standard, to 35 per cent. Photographs were reduced to a commodity on the supermarket shelves. Finally Getty wound up in 2014 giving away millions of pictures free of charge, their contributors paid nothing and powerless to resist. Free that is for editorial and academic use on the web, and only on the web, but – linked straight back to Getty. Why? Destroying the competition, yes, but also turning their new 'customers' into advertising targets – Peter Krogh unearths the clue:

> Getty Images (or third parties acting on its behalf) may collect data related to use of the Embedded Viewer and embedded Getty Images Content, and reserves the right to place advertisements in the Embedded Viewer or otherwise monetize its use without any compensation to you. (4)

As they say, if it's free, you are the product. Getty is under pressure from the new owners, Carlyle, and data may now be their oil of the future. (5).

As Sarah Nuttall writes, "Data is the oil of the 21st Century. Which is ironic. Mark Getty, founder and former owner of Getty Images once famously said that intellectual property was the oil of the 21st Century. Not anymore in the company that bears his name. Now Getty Images is owned by a private equity firm. They paid $3.3bn for Getty. They need a return on their investment and images alone just don't bring in that kind of cash." (6).

Meanwhile Gates, who had bought the vast Bettmann Archive of 16 million images, found he had bitten off far more than he could chew and mothballed it deep inside the Iron Mountain Corporation's old limestone mine, in an underground refrigerated cave. At least there it's securely archived and accessible, which is more than can be said by those national papers, blind to the commercial, never mind the historical, value of work built up over decades, who created space by chucking it out with the rubbish. Then Corbis blundered into a world they could neither understand nor control. They bought up French news agency, Sygma, without realising that at Sygma it was the photographers who owned their pictures.

According to *Editorial Photographers UK & Ireland* (EPUK):

> However, it appears that Bill Gates and the Corbis
> management are greatly mistaken in their assessment
> of the situation – they thought that by buying the
> Sygma agency, they would automatically become the
> owners of the archives. But this is not the case, as
> French law protects photographers in France, which
> contrary to the US copyright law, makes the
> photographers the owners of their images for life. (7)

Corbis then tried to entangle the photographers contractually, proposed redundancies, provoked a strike, and spiralled downwards losing millions to the point where, after facing a court award of about $1.84 for losing 750 originals belonging to one of the Sygma photographers, in 2010 Corbis Sygma finally declared bankruptcy in France. (8)

European copyright law is – different. Countries within the European tradition of Authors' Rights make it much more difficult to divest authors of their ownership than is the case in the Anglo-Saxon jurisdictions such as the UK and the USA. When it comes to fighting media titans, Europe points the way.

Of all the European countries, Germany offers the best protection. In Germany copyright is inalienable. Clients cannot demand or extract it, photographers cannot sell it. Moreover German fair contract law is developing the principle that sale of extended rights must command increased fees. Combining the two, photographers over there retain not only ownership but also a considerable degree of control over their work. So when a German company such as the Bauer Media Group comes over here trying to force British photographers to surrender their copyright, they still have to behave themselves back home. (9) They publish in 15 countries around the world, and if all those other jurisdictions measured up to German standards, the concentration of ownership worldwide would be greatly reduced.

There are two ways to resist big media power over intellectual property. The best, and the simplest, though not sufficient in itself, is through the retention of copyright ownership and control by the individual photographers themselves, as in Germany. I would say that, wouldn't I, I'm a working photographer – but this would not only be of benefit to photographers. It is also the best way of preserving our heritage, as we won't be throwing our life's work into a skip, or burying it down a mineshaft. And the best way of ensuring in future there will still be professionals able to earn a living while creating photographs. All it requires is the political will. The reforms of 1988 require completing. By making copyright the inalienable right of the author, and by making copyright licences here in the UK subject to fair contract law. This requires no foresight, no vision. It is not a fantasy. It is not impractical.

It is already a working everyday reality, plain for all to see – but not here in the UK. Yet.

This was the last thing on the minds of the copyright 'modernisers' of recent years, starting with Gowers who began his 2006 Review by declaring: "I do not think the system is in need of radical overhaul." Before then going on to make very radical and damaging proposals such as Orphan Works legislation. (10) So much for creators' rights! Nor was protecting these the aim of the civil servants in the Intellectual Property Office, or as some would say, the Intellectual Property Obliteration Office, drafting the ensuing copyright legislation and playing Yes Minister to both Labour and then Coalition governments. Instead the goal was Economic Growth, a mirage in the desert of austerity. According to the 2011 Hargreaves Review, a classic case of policy based evidence, reducing – yes, reducing – the control of creators was to create billions of pounds of growth per year. A ludicrous claim demolished by, amongst others, Andrew Orlowski of The Register : "The IPO's economic 'evidence' in support of the Hargreaves conclusions was cobbled together in a hurry, with fantastically implausible figures plucked out of the air."(11) You'd have thought that, as the creative sector is crucial to the future growth of the UK economy, and protecting the creators crucial to the growth of the creative sector, radical reform was indeed needed – to ensure that creators could continue to earn a living through exercising their rights.

Photographers did not give up without a fight. Our spirited resistance knocked the guts out of the IPO's first attack, Clause 43 of the Digital Economy Bill 2010 (12), but we could not prevent their second attempt in the Enterprise and Regulatory Reform Act 2013. We could only limit the damage.

Nevertheless some protection was in fact won. An inspired NUJ proposal for a small claims court for copyright cases has resulted in the new small claims track through the Intellectual Property Enterprise Court. And the launching of the Copyright Hub (13) for connecting clients with rights holders may, depending on how it develops, allow creators to deal direct, by-passing the titans. But since 2006 the fundamental question of ownership by creators of their intellectual property rights has been repeatedly and deliberately evaded. It will take a fresh generation of politicians to get to the heart of the matter.

The only other way to deal with concentrated ownership is to break it up. Or at the very least, prevent further corporate acquisition. This too requires political will. And while it appears a labour of Sisyphus, in 2010 something rather remarkable happened. When Getty tried to buy up Rex Features, one of its few remaining competitors in the UK, a referral to the Competition Commission by the Office of Fair Trading was enough to succeed where others had failed, or even failed to try.

The OFT referred the proposed deal to the Competition Commission for further investigation, arguing that there was a 'realistic prospect of a substantial lessening of competition'. Amelia Fletcher, senior director of mergers at the OFT, said: "A number of publishers, the key customers in this market, are concerned about the potential impact of the acquisition." (14)

And so the Getty steamroller was at last brought to a halt. Yes, just the once. But, another world is not entirely beyond the bounds of possibility.

Notes

(1)   Ownership of photographs according to the CDPA 1988 (*www.ipo.gov.uk/cdpact1988.pdf*): 11 First ownership of copyright (1) The author of a work is the first owner of any copyright in it, subject to (2) Where a literary, dramatic, musical or artistic work, or a film, is made by an employee in the course of his employment, his employer is the first owner of any copyright in the work subject to any agreement to the contrary.

(2)   See the CDPA 1988, 11 (2) – as above

(3)   See Editorial Photographers UK & Ireland (EPUK): *www.epuk.org/First-Person/16/inside-the-scotsman-dispute*

(4)   Peter Krogh, Getty Did What? (*http://thedambook.com/getty-did-what?*)

(5)   *www.carlyle.com/*

(6)   *www.sarahnuttallcopywriter.co.uk/blog/Getty-Images-Go-Free*

(7)   See again EPUK: *www.epuk.org/News/123/sygma-the-death-of-an-agency*

(8)   *www.amateurphotographer.co.uk/photo-news/535000/photographers-face-two-year-wait-for-sygma-photos*

(9)   See the 2010 Bauer case: *www.londonfreelance.org/fl/1006grab.html?i=flindex&d=2010_06*

(10)   Stop 43. *www.stop43.org.uk* The best place to start to understand the implications of this and related proposals for 'Extended Collective Licensing', 'Exceptions', and the UK's photographic copyright wars from the Digital Economy Act 2010 to the Enterprise and Regulatory Reform Act 2013.

(11)   See *www.theregister.co.uk/2011/11/17/ipo_quilty_select_committee*

(12)   See again Stop 43, *www.stop43.org.uk/pages/our_history.html*

(13)   See *www.copyrighthub.co.uk*

(14)   See *www.theguardian.com/media/2010/jul/08/getty-images-rex-features-oft*

The business of books

Granville Williams

Book publishing rarely makes front-page news, but the size of the merger of Random House (owned by the German media group Bertelsmann) and Penguin (owned by Pearson) in October 2013 sent shock waves through Western publishing circles and generated a spate of newspaper and radio reports analysing its significance. It reduced the 'Big Six' to the 'Big Five' global trade book publishers and created the world's largest publisher, Penguin Random House, which will control 25 per cent of the worldwide consumer book market and nearly 30 per cent in the USA. Rupert Murdoch, whose News Corporation owns the book publisher HarperCollins, made a late, unsuccessful 'spoiler' cash bid, reported to be £1.6 billion, for Penguin when news of the planned merger became public.

The sheer scale of the merger stood in sharp contrast with the world of publishing in which Allen Lane launched his first ten Penguin Books in August 1935 and began to have a major impact on the cultural and political life of Britain. The day after his death in July 1970, however, the merger of Penguin and Pearson Longman was announced, part of the pattern of consolidation in book publishing which has led to the creation of the 'Big Five'. The other groups are listed here but future consolidation is likely to reduce the number even further.

The Hachette Book Group (HBG) is a division of the second largest trade and educational book publisher in the world, Hachette Livre, which is based in France and is a subsidiary of the French media company, Lagardère. The company acquired the Time Warner Book group for $537 million in 2006 and changed the name of Warner Books to Grand Central Publishing. In the US it also has imprints like Little, Brown & Company; in the UK Gollancz, Hodder & Stoughton and Weidenfeld and Nicolson.

HarperCollins Publishers is a subsidiary of News Corp, the global media company led by Rupert Murdoch. In the US, News Corp acquired Harper & Row in 1987 and in 1990, the UK publisher William Collins & Sons to form the worldwide book group. In May 2014 HarperCollins purchased the Canadian-based publisher of romantic titles, Harlequin, for £246 million. Approximately 40 percent of Harlequin's revenues come from books published in languages other than English. The company publishes in 34 languages while 99 per cent of HarperCollins books are published in English. Robert Thomson, News Corp's chief executive, said, "It vastly expands our digital platform, extending our reach across borders and languages...and is a significant step in our strategy to establish a network of digital properties in the growth regions of the world."

Macmillan is owned by the German Company Holtzbrinck, with imprints in the United States, Germany, the United Kingdom, Australia, South Africa, and around the world. Macmillan U.S. trade book publishers include Farrar, Straus and Giroux; Henry Holt and Company; Picador; St. Martin's Press; in the UK, Pan, Picador and Sidgwick & Jackson.

Simon & Schuster was founded in 1924 and is currently the publishing arm of the media company CBS Corporation. Its publishing divisions include Free Press and Scribner.

Since the 1960s the rise of large international book publishing conglomerates has transformed the landscape of the book trade. Andrè Schiffrin began working in American publishing in 1956 when there was, both in the US and the UK, a plethora of small independent publishing houses. He first worked for a mass market paperback house, the New American Library, which was owned and inspired by Penguin Books. He then moved to Pantheon in 1962. Schiffrin points out, "In Europe and America, publishing has a long tradition as an intellectually and politically engaged profession. Publishers have always prided themselves on their ability to balance the imperative of making money with that of issuing worthwhile books." (1)

These publishers were satisfied with profits of three to four percent, but, from the 1960s on, a number of factors saw the rise of publishing corporations. The first was, as with Allen Lane, many of the individuals who ran these publishing houses, people with clear views on what they wanted to publish, were by the 1960s thinking about retiring and the sale or merger of their firms was often the only alternative. Between the 1960s and today there were two phases in this consolidation.

John B. Thompson's chapter, 'The Emergence of Publishing Corporations', in *Merchants of Culture* gives a clear account of this process. (2) The first phase, in the 1960s and 1970s saw the active involvement in the publishing field of large corporations with substantial stakes in information, entertainment, education and the emerging computer industry. For these companies the publishing houses fitted neatly into what was a dominant business strategy and concept, 'synergy', where books could be turned into movies or turned into content for 'teaching machines'. Thompson points out:

> The idea of 'synergy', whether it was between different media formats or between equipment ('hardware') and content ('software'), provided a compelling and

seemingly cogent management rationale for large corporations to acquire publishing houses; it was a powerful pull factor. (3)

Synergy turned out to be a myth, but another reason why large US corporations became disillusioned with publishing houses was their modest profitability, often below 10 per cent, in comparison with scientific, technical and medical publishing sectors where profit margins were 20 per cent and more. The giant electronics corporation RCA, for example, purchased Random House in 1965 and sold it in 1980.

In the early 1980s other factors put pressure on the re- maining independent publishers: they were being squeezed out by market forces. The growth of retail chains (Barnes and Noble, Borders, Waterstones) meant that the volume of sales for bestselling titles increased dramatically, but also the costs and risks. Agents played a more central role, and bidding for potential best sellers meant the scale of advances excluded independent publishers. Selling to large corporations was a means of survival for publishers unable to compete on their own.

Another important factor was that whilst large media corporations in the US sought to divest themselves of their publishing houses, French (Hachette Livre) and German media conglomerates (Bertelsmann and Holtsbrinck) were interested in expanding beyond their own domestic markets and acquiring American and English publishing houses in order to get access to global English-speaking markets. Also UK publishers like Pearson wanted to build their stake in the US market. This has resulted in the ownership structure for book publishing we have today, a state of affairs which prompted Ian Jack, former editor of Granta, to observe:

How can it be that Penguin, one of the most innovative publishing companies in the world, ends up in the hands of a German firm that, 50 years ago, was only a quarter of Penguin's size, with an unenviable publishing record? More generally, how is it that so many British publishers are owned in Germany and France, given that the English language is one of this country's last great assets, and we should surely know more about its exploitation than others do? (4)

The damaged ecology of the book business

"I grew up in a world in which many parts together formed a community adversarial in a microscopic way but communal in a larger sense: authors, editors, agents, publishers, wholesalers, retailers and readers. I hope...that we do not look back one day...and only see what has become a largely denuded wasteland." Peter Mayer, Overlook Press (5)

Independent publishers still exist in the UK, with companies like Bloomsbury, Faber and Granta holding on to seven per cent of the market, but the ecology of the book business, from the search for new authors, through to publication, distribution and sales is under severe threat in the US and UK not only from the disruptive dominance of Amazon but also the consequences of policies pursued or supported by the giant publishers and the chain bookstores in the past.

In the mid-to-late 1990s when online bookselling was in its infancy, book chains like Barnes and Noble and Borders in the US and Waterstones (which later absorbed Dillons and Ottakers) and Borders in the UK were expanding and offering deeply discounted items made possible by favourable publishers' terms not extended to independents.

Two decades ago in the US there were about 4,000 independent booksellers, now only about 1,900 remain. Manhattan, which in the post-war years had some 333 bookstores, had barely 30 in 2010, a number since reduced with the closure of the Borders book chain. In the UK the number of independent bookshops has fallen below 1,000 in 2013 for the first time as a combination of Amazon, e-books and High Street rent increases put them out of business. However the chains themselves are now imperilled. Borders has gone; Waterstones, owned by WH Smith, then HMV, until several poor results led to its sale to Russian billionaire Alexander Mamut in May 2011, struggles on. Persistent rumours that Barnes & Noble wants to sell its 1,332 stores keep surfacing.

The remorseless consolidation of book publishing has also provoked specific criticisms about the imperatives of sales and profitability produced by the pressure within these large corporations for growth and market share. Instead of nurturing and supporting authors as they develop, the emphasis shifts to short term success. The result is the publishing output of the large houses becomes more homogeneous, more commercial and more closely tied to celebrity and entertainment, whist good literature and serious non-fiction is increasingly marginalized.

This was the view of André Schriffin (he died in December 2013) drawing on his rich experience in publishing. When RCA decided to unload Random House, a multibillionaire media owner, S.I. Newhouse, acquired the publisher. In 1989 Newhouse installed Alberto Vitale to run Pantheon. Vitale told Schriffin that his policy was that each book should make money on its own and that one title should no longer be allowed to subsidise another. But Vitale went further, saying Pantheon should stop publishing "so many books on the left" and instead publish more on the right. Schriffin resigned as editor-in-chief in March 1990, along with most of his senior editorial team, in protest at this narrow and destructive approach. He later argued:

Books today have become mere adjuncts to the world
of the mass media, offering light entertainment and
reassurances that all is for the best in this, the best of
all possible worlds. The resulting control of the
spread of ideas is stricter than anyone would have

thought possible in a free society. The need for public debate and open discussion, inherent in the democratic ideal, conflicts with the ever-stricter demand for total profit. (5)

The counter-argument to this view is worth considering. In the US 290,000 titles were published in 2011; in the UK just under 150,000 (the figures include professional and scholarly books). On the surface such a proliferation of titles suggests that the consolidation of the large publishing houses has gone hand in hand with a huge expansion of titles produced by smaller publishing houses and therefore the sheer number and range of books being published contradicts the idea that the corporatisation of the publishing business poses a threat to literary culture.

We need to consider two kinds of diversity here: diversity of output and diversity in the marketplace. The important issue is not, Thompson argues, ."..the diversity or otherwise of the books that are published, but rather the diversity or otherwise of the books that are noticed, purchased and read." He analyses the sales bands for books published between 2002-2006 and finds, ."..the market is concentrating on a small number of books that sell well, indeed better than ever, whereas the number of books that sell in modest but acceptable quantities is declining." He concludes that, ."..despite the enormous volume and diversity of output, the marketplace for books is increasingly one in which the winners take more and everything else faces a harder and harder struggle to get noticed, bought and read." (6)

The Random House/Penguin merger was essentially defensive, an attempt to resist the predations of digital competition, mainly from Amazon, by rationalising the costs of production, warehousing, shipping and accounting across the two companies. Such mergers are standard (but not always successful) business practices but this one prompted comment about the impact such massive changes will have on authors when the merged company will be publishing 5,000 titles a year under 250 separate imprints.

The Society of Authors is worried that writers with modest sales will fall down the priority list. Nicola Solomon, the society's chief executive, said, "As publishers get bigger, it may not be economical to support authors selling 2,000 or 3,000 titles, or promote the back catalogue. My guess is that they are more likely to put their money into something that might make a super-profit for the 'something new or sexy' that might be a runaway success." (7)

The Amazon effect

"Amazon has successfully fostered the idea that a book is a thing of minimal value—it's a widget." Dennis Johnson, independent publisher.

Joseph Schumpeter identified the 'perennial gale of creative destruction' that sweeps through economies as innovative insurgents take on entrenched incumbents. Regional and national newspapers along with travel agents and record labels, publishers and booksellers have been pulverized by the impact on what seemed to be invulnerable business models by Google, Apple and Amazon.

In 1995, Jeff Bezos started Amazon. He realized, before Google and Facebook, that the greatest value of an online company was the ability to gather vast amounts of personal information on individual customers. It wasn't his love of books that led Bezos to start an online bookstore but books as a product. They were easy to distribute and hard to break, and there was a major distribution warehouse in Oregon to draw on.

George Packer, in a recent analysis of Amazon for *The New Yorker* found the company difficult to write about – it would not confirm facts as simple as how many employees it has in Seattle or how many Kindles it has sold. He observes, "It's impossible to know for sure, but, according to one publisher's estimate, book sales in the U.S. now make up no more than seven per cent of the company's roughly seventy-five billion dollars in annual revenue." (8)

Amazon is still very actively involved in the book business and its sheer scale and predatory power concerns publishers. Amazon used to employ writers to comment on books and their merits but that era is long gone with editorial suggestions for readers replaced with algorithms that used customers' history to make recommendations for future purchases.

Indeed everything at Amazon is driven by data and algorithms. This, however, is far from a neutral and scientific process. The results generated by Amazon's search engine are partly determined by promotional fees paid by publishers. Amazon extracts all sorts of payments from publishers so that its percentage discount on books is in the mid-fifties. Random House currently gives Amazon an effective discount of around 53 per cent. For a smaller house, Amazon's total discount can go as high as 60 per cent, which cuts deeply into already slim profit margins.

In his book *The Everything Store: Jeff Bezos and the Age of Amazon* Brad Stone describes one campaign to exert pressure for better terms from smaller publishers. It was known internally as the 'gazelle project' after Bezos suggested that, "Amazon should approach these small publishers the way a cheetah would pursue a sickly gazelle."

Whilst Amazon was still pushing CDs, Apple had taken control of the digital music market and Bezos did not want the same thing to happen to books. This led to the Kindle. "Your job is to kill your own business," Bezos told the engineer in charge. "I want you to proceed as if your goal is to put everyone selling physical books out of a job."

In late 2007, at a press conference in New York, Bezos unveiled the Kindle, a simple, lightweight device that could store as many as 200 books, downloaded from Amazon's 3G network. Bezos announced that the price of best-sellers and new titles would be $9.99, regardless of length or quality. The price was below wholesale in some cases, and so low that it represented a serious threat to the market for hardcover sales which Barnes & Noble and independent booksellers relied on.

Amazon knew it would lose money when people bought the Kindle, but make money when they used it – by buying e-books from Amazon. By 2010, Amazon controlled 90 per cent of the market in digital books – a dominance that almost no company, in any industry, could claim. Its prohibitively low prices warded off competition.

When the 'Big Six' major US publishers attempted to create an electronic bookstore with Apple, Amazon complained to the US Department of Justice, arguing that the publishers were conspiring to raise prices for electronic books in violation of antitrust law. Amazon won but as Apple and the publishers see it, the ruling ignored the context of the case that when the key events occurred, Amazon effectively had a monopoly in digital books and was selling them so cheaply that it resembled predatory pricing – a barrier to entry for potential competitors. Since then, Amazon's share of the e-book market in the US has dropped to about 65 per cent, with the rest going largely to Apple and to Barnes & Noble, which sells the Nook e-reader.

Amazon demonstrates a drive towards dominance in online retailing, even buying up potential online competitors before they become a threat. As one US bookseller observed, "Monopolies are always problematic in a free society, and they are more so when they are dealing with the dissemination of ideas, which is what book publishing is about...Amazon simply has too much power in the marketplace. And when their business interest conflicts with the public interest, the public interest suffers." (9)

Bezos celebrates his disruptive impact, scorns the old elitist publishing gatekeepers and enthusiastically promotes e-publishing which gives people the opportunity to self-publish and eliminate the gatekeepers. Packer concludes his *New Yorker* piece, "But gatekeepers are also barriers against the complete commercialization of ideas, allowing new talent the time to develop and learn to tell difficult truths. When the last gatekeeper but one is gone, will Amazon care whether a book is any good?"

Policy Issues

Amazon dominates the online-retail and e-book market in many countries. In the UK Amazon Anonymous has a campaign to alert people to Amazon's business and employment practices, but the big issue is what governments, the European Union (EU), and antitrust authorities will do. The digital giants like Amazon and Google are becoming too powerful, and public concern about this is growing.

The response of the internet giants has been to ratchet up their spending on lobbying to protect their long-term interests in Washington and the EU. For example, it was revealed in November 2013 that Amazon was involved in writing a large number of amendments to the EU's new data protection law and convinced a number of MEPs to submit these amendments, hoping that they would be adopted by the European Parliament. One of the Amazon documents included 41 pages of amendments to the proposed law. (10) This massive copy-pasting of industry-drafted amendments caused major controversy, because it essentially gave large corporations the power to co-write EU laws. That is why we need to wake up to the sheer predatory power of the new titans of the online world whose imperatives are to grow and achieve dominance in their chosen markets.

Notes

(1)   Andrè Schiffrin, *The Business of Books,* Verso, 2000, p5

(2)   John B. Thompson, *Merchants of Culture: The Publishing Business in the Twenty-First Century,* Polity, 2010.

(3)   Ibid, p104

(4)   Ian Jack, 'What does Penguin's merger with Random House say about Britain?', *The Guardian,* 27 July 2013.

(4)   Quoted in Steve Wassermann, 'The Amazon Effect', *The Nation,* 29 May 2012.

(5)   Schiffrin, op.cit. p 91 & p152.

(6)   Thompson, op.cit pp 386-394. This is a very bald summary of the author's argument.

(7)   Jennifer Rankin, 'Plot thickens for authors as merger of titans creates publishing powerhouse', *The Observer,* 24 July, 2013.

(8)   George Packer, 'Cheap Words: Amazon is good for customers but is it good for books?' *The New Yorker,* 17 February 2014.

(9)   Quoted in Wasserman, op. cit.

(10)   Corporate Europe Observatory, 29 November 2013, at: *http://corporateeurope.org/lobbycracy/2013/11/amazon-lobbying-weaken-data-privacy-rights-refusing-lobby-transparency*

Policies for UK media plurality
Jonathan Hardy

Calls for the break-up of large media groups have met with little success in the UK. Official policy has instead relaxed rules on media ownership. The widespread belief among policy-makers that any remaining problems were diminishing in an expanding digital universe bolstered long-standing calls for liberalisation.

So 2010-11 marked something of a reversal. Media concentration was brought back to the spotlight, first by News Corporation's bid for BSkyB, then by the setting up of the Leveson Inquiry, which investigated the toxic fusion of media ownership, media power and political influence across the British establishment. (1)We are still inside this critical moment and the historic opportunity it affords to redraw communications policy. But there are serious efforts underway to limit the scope of any new measures on media plurality. So we must ask and answer the old questions in new circumstances: should there be action to tackle problems arising from media ownership and control? Does it matter if there isn't? An unwilling government and reluctant regulator meet powerful industry interests keen to retain as much of the status quo as possible. The opposition Labour Party may yet link media to the wider themes of unaccountable corporate power, but knows it would face the wrath of an already hostile press before a knife-edge General Election. It is up to media reformers, trade unionists, media and cultural workers and users, civil society groups and supporters to demand bold action. This chapter explores the sorry state of media ownership policy and outlines why action is needed, but it also makes a case for new thinking and approaches to tackle 21st century problems.

The sorry state of media ownership policies

The UK had a concentrated press decades before any policy action to remedy the situation was formulated by government. During the mid 20th century anti-monopoly controls were introduced for the national and regional press, but, with a few exceptions, failed to curb increasing concentration. The other main policy action came through broadcasting legislation, setting rules on ownership of commercial television licences that were extended to include cross-ownership between television and newspapers. The third key element was the maintenance of the BBC and public service television as a regulated system designed to deliver 'internal pluralism'.

All the media ownership rules came under mounting waves of attack from the early 1980s, although they were defended and some have been retained in modified form up to the present. Successive Broadcasting Acts extended ownership rules to new platforms and services but generally relaxed ownership caps affecting existing market players. Attacked by media companies, advertisers, organised industry bodies and market liberal policy-makers, media ownership rules were condemned as rigid and obsolescent. They prevented businesses growing to a sufficient size to compete globally, stave off predatory foreign acquisition, and build the capacity to deliver investments in digital technologies. With the growth of the Internet, convergent media companies argued that there was no longer a need for regulatory intervention since markets were opening up and delivering digital pluralism. News publishers and other groups argued that amidst expanding media markets, they needed greater consolidation to withstand the stormy waves of creative destruction wrought by digitalisation and the rerouting of advertising revenues online.

UK communications legislation was successively, if cautiously, deregulatory, from the 1990 and 1996 Broadcasting Acts to the 2003 Communications Act. The imperatives have been on opening up media markets, promoting light touch regulation and stimulating growth. The Communications Act 2003 relaxed rules on ITV ownership. It established the infamous 'Murdoch clause' by removing the restriction on ownership of Channel 5 by newsgroups whose share of the national news market was 20 per cent or more.

Since the 2003 Act there have been no restrictions on foreign ownership. Richard Desmond bought the terrestrial, public service Channel 5 for £103.5m from German broadcaster RTL in 2010 and sold it in May 2014 for £450 million to the US media group Viacom, one of the top five global media groups. There are no limits on ownership share for any single media proprietor except as may be imposed in a merger situation or a possible competition investigation. Advertising agencies can own radio and TV stations. As Will Hutton explained, despite our long history of democracy, Britain is lagging behind. "We impose no nationality requirement. We do not tightly police the share of any media market held by one proprietor, nor make demands about limiting owners' power to take ownership chunks across the media domains; we do not even care much about preventing market dominance. The assumption has been that lightly applied competition law, along with self-regulation, is all that is required, with little thought for any political and cultural consequences." (2)

By the time the Conservative-led coalition government replaced New Labour in 2010 a broad policy consensus had emerged. Market mechanisms and digitalisation would deliver increasing media diversity and responsiveness to consumers. Where problems of market power remained, intervening to tackle these by means of ownership limits was neither appropriate nor effective. In place of halted steps towards a new Communications Act, government policy instead favoured business support for the creative industries, measures to curb the BBC, and action to shrink Ofcom's resources and file down its teeth.

This course was interrupted. News Corporation's bid for BSkyB triggered concern about an unprecedented level of concentration of media power that would occur in the supposedly pluralising media markets of digital TV and news. The bid also threw a spotlight on the arrangements for handling media mergers. During the passage of the Communications Bill, Lord Puttnam and others had succeeded in placing a public interest test into the merger regime. This was intended to ensure that concerns about diversity of supply in news and broadcasting could be addressed when they arose in media mergers. While the European Commission approved the News Corp-BSkyB bid on competition grounds, Business Secretary Vince Cable called on Ofcom to carry out a public interest test. The resulting process highlighted limitations and drew calls for reform from media companies and campaign groups alike. The Government exploited the restrictive legal framing of the public interest test to rule out not only consideration of 'fit and proper' governance but also a host of other concerns about the power and behaviour of Murdoch's media empire to exercise market dominance from 'triple-play' TV-broadband-telephony subscriptions, to film and sports rights, to corporate cross-promotion. But it was the controversial power given to the Secretary of State that lifted the issue from the specialist policy domain to public scrutiny. When Cable resigned following unguarded comments made in a sting operation conducted by the Telegraph, the Conservative Jeremy Hunt was required to make the quasi-judicial decision on the BSkyB merger. How could a minister in a newly-elected government supported by Murdoch's papers demonstrate sufficient impartiality? In fact, Hunt was days away from approving the deal, involving the decoupling of Sky News, when the phone-hacking scandal reignited, and News Corp. withdrew.

It was that scandal and its aftermath that did most to shift the policy ground, highlighting problems of media power and returning media plurality back to prominence. The Leveson Report called for a new system for measuring and addressing concentration of media ownership, but offered few concrete recommendations. However, since then there has been a Government-commissioned Ofcom consultation and report on measuring plurality, a House of Lords Communications Committee investigation, and a Department for Culture, Media and Sport (DCMS) government review. (3) The CPBF gave evidence to all three, but the formal proposals that have emerged so far from both Ofcom and the Lords fall far short of our calls for action. Before assessing these responses, though, it is important to consider the scale of the problems that need to be solved.

Media power problems in the digital age

With an enormously expanded range of communication services surely the problems of media ownership and control have diminished? The DCMS review thinks so, claiming that barriers to market entry have lowered so that emerging digital markets can deliver much of the plurality needed by themselves. On the contrary, the impact of digitalisation on media industries, while profound, has been uneven. There are still barriers and advantages that favour large providers of 'legacy' media, as well as scale and network effects that favour new digital giants such as Google, Apple, Facebook and Twitter. (4) There are advantages for large firms over newcomers in high-cost content creation activities like regular professional news. While markets are volatile there are advantages for vertically integrated companies over competitors and for those who can benefit from economies of scale and scope, from factors that help to lock in consumers (sunk investment in equipment and contract services, etc.) and from cross-promotion and other economies of synergy. (5) Some sectors such as news publishing are certainly threatened, creating opportunities for new entrants, but most of the latter are either undercapitalised, or advertising vehicles, or are cross-subsidised by other businesses. The trends, evident in the US, are likely to become more apparent in the UK. News is becoming a division within large multimedia corporations who are presiding over a disinvestment of resources in news-gathering, with profound consequences for democracy. (6)

In the UK today, three companies control some 70 per cent of daily national newspaper circulation, the five largest regional newspaper publishers control 70 per cent of circulation, just four companies have an almost 80 per cent share of the commercial radio market, while one news wholesaler provides bulletins for the vast majority of those stations. Richard Desmond's Northern and Shell, owns Channel 5, four national newspapers, celebrity magazines such as OK! and Portland TV which runs 17 UK broadcast channels with carriage on Sky, Freeview, Virgin and BT Vision and includes adult channels such as Television X and Red Hot TV. All employees know they must cross-promote the business empire, with the anti-immigration, neoliberal editorial agendas of the Express and Daily Star informing a string of Channel 5 programmes like *Gypsies on Benefits* and *Proud*.

A handful of owners in the national and regional press has a large market share allowing a disproportionate influence over the media agenda, public debate and political opinion. The case advanced for such consolidation was that it would offer the prospect of substantial economies of scale and cost-efficient operation. Instead, according to the National Union of Journalists, the impact of consolidation on local newspapers and local radio has been a narrowing of the range and diversity of editorial voices and massive job cuts, with regional hubs covering 'local' reporting across a number of titles.

Some argue that while 'legacy' publications remain under concentrated ownership, the growth of online publication means that plurality concerns, and the case for intervention, has diminished. Yet, it would be wrong to conclude that the massively increased availability of content online diminishes concern about the sources and supply of news, or the share and reach of media companies operating across various platforms. As Ofcom has highlighted, 'traditional media providers account for 10 of the top 15 online providers of news (eight newspaper groups plus the BBC and Sky), with the remainder predominantly being news aggregators rather than alternative sources of news'. (7) While supply of information has vastly increased, there remains a lack of what is called 'exposure diversity'. Networked communications have transformed the capacity for messages to be exchanged. Yet problems of scarcity and control remain evident.

Plurality policies and media reform

If markets don't simply deliver media plurality and intervention is needed, what should be done? Some have proposed a cap on ownership either for the total media market (variously defined), or in specific sub-sectors. Enders Analysis proposes a cap on total media market revenues of 15 per cent for any single firm. This is simple and impactful. However, total market calculations like Enders' that include wider sectors such as all publishing and computer games are problematic as they would permit significant concentrations within sub-sectors like news publishing, television and radio services before total market thresholds were met. In addition, defining the market by revenue would not provide a sufficiently sensitive instrument to identify problems of market and media power.

The CPBF has proposed a more compound approach that involves:

• A total market threshold for media content services across UK television, newspapers and periodical publishing, radio and online.

• Thresholds in key markets for news and markets for media content services.

• Powers for the regulator to carry out a public interest test when market thresholds were reached, by periodic review, and on other grounds.

The CPBF proposals, adopted by the TUC and, in modified form, by the Media Reform Coalition have been described as hybrid, as they combine market caps with investigations that can result in other action than simply the breakup of firms. The CPBF proposes that the public interest (PI) test, established by the Communications Act 2003, should be revised and extended. It can provide a key means of helping to secure media pluralism across converging media, and extending obligations to commercial media firms that have a significant reach and influence. The proposals are guided by a key principle: for media that serve public audiences, with size and reach come responsibilities. The old approaches do need overhauling but the principle should be that providers with significant market share meet requirements and obligations to safeguard communication rights.

Fixed caps alone are regarded as too restrictive and cumbersome in changing market conditions. The CPBF agrees, and proposes that market share should serve as a guide for triggering investigations that would consider plurality concerns as they arise across local, national and supranational media markets. Firms with a large share in news and other media markets should have to meet public interest requirements or face possible divestment. At the light end such requirements would include compliance with relevant industry codes of conduct, measures to safeguard editorial independence and prevent editors being sacked at the whim of owners; at the stronger end they would include undertakings to ensure greater plurality, for instance, by sharing resources with other suppliers or community users. A news organisation might have public duties to sustain investment in news-gathering or meet undertakings to pool and share resources with other media providers where this benefits pluralism. At the stronger end too would be requirements to establish new forms of public governance. In particular we think that the maximum market share for privately owned media in key markets should be 30 per cent. Above that, the company would either need to divest or reorganise the service to comply with public interest requirements – for instance by establishing a public trust or community enterprise.

We now have responses to these proposals. The Lords Communications Committee Report on media plurality offers tentative steps forward. The Committee affirms the importance of plurality, agrees that it raises different concerns from those addressed in competition regulation, and concludes that plurality must address digital intermediaries as well as content providers. It accepts advice that the BBC should not be subject to new 'control measures' whose purpose is to sustain plurality beyond the public service system, and it strongly rejects top-slicing the licence fee. All that is very welcome.

The key proposal is that the regulator Ofcom should be given a statutory responsibility to conduct plurality reviews every four to five years. The Secretary of State can reject Ofcom's report and proposals but must give reasons for doing so. For 'media transactions' (mergers or take-overs), the power to decide should be taken away from the Secretary of State altogether. The Committee recommends that Ofcom investigates plurality, the Competition Commission investigates competition issues, and the Ofcom Board gives the final decision.

The Lords committee broadly rejected both fixed ownership caps, or the CPBF's 'hybrid' approach. It did so in part on the politically pragmatic grounds that there is a lack of consensus on public interest obligations across industry. In fact, the CPBF proposals anticipate and accommodate such differences. However, the opposition to even Leveson-compliant self-regulation from amongst powerful commercial media may have been enough to convince the Committee to duck the challenge. Ownership caps also contravene the committee's stated principle that 'the assessment of plurality should drive the decision about which remedy or intervention is appropriate, not the other way around'. Yet the rejection of caps is highly problematic.

To be clear, a system without caps could work. The Committee proposes that Parliament lay down in statute 'narrative' guidelines on what constitutes sufficient pluralism for Ofcom to follow. The problem is that the approach proposed is highly discretionary, rules out divestment in all but 'exceptional' circumstances, and lacks publicly accountable safeguards. Thresholds for action and caps based on market share, audience share or other measurements have limitations and should not be the only route to action, but they do provide a level of transparency and certainty for citizens and market players alike. That contrasts with the real risks of opaque deal-making, or worse, protracted litigation, between industry players, regulators and government. After decades of inaction it is time to move to a system that can instil public confidence. One requirement for that is to bring the public properly into regulation, something the CPBF advocated, but the report entirely ignores. Ofcom should be required to have regard for evidence of 'significant public concern' and to initiate pubic interest tests in response as one of the triggers for action. Public involvement has been the vital missing component in communications regulation; public concern needs to be placed at the heart of democratic media policy-making.

The other major problem concerns scope. In future, the Lords Committee and Ofcom both argue, plurality policy 'should be limited to the activities of media enterprises engaged in news and current affairs content'. (8) Everyone agrees that plurality matters most in news. Many academics and indeed campaigners support this as focusing on what is simple, do-able and may have the best chance of tangible results. It is a strong case, but there are problems. Shrinking plurality to news would narrow action even beyond the scope of the current public interest test, which includes the quality and range of broadcasting services. We must ask: does supply across the range of commercial communication content and services involve problems of control, editorial influence, content diversity, and access? Would it matter for media plurality if 21st Century Fox bought the 61 per cent of BSkyB that Murdoch does not own? The CPBF believes it would, and will continue to call for a much broader pluralism policy capable of addressing when media power and market power work together to the detriment of entertainment, sports, culture, content and communications services as well as news.

Notes

(1)   Leveson Inquiry, *An inquiry into the culture, practices and ethics of the press*, 2012. Available online: *http://www.official-documents.gov.uk/document/nc1213/hc07/0780*

(2)   W. Hutton, 'What the Coulson affair tells us about Murdoch's lust for power', *The Observer*, 5 September, 2010. Available at *http://www.guardian.co.uk/commentisfree/2010/sep/05/coulson-murdoch-phone-tapping?CMP=twt_gu* (accessed 27 September 2010)

(3)   House of Lords Communications Committee, Media Plurality, HL Paper 120, 2014. Available at *http://www.publications.parliament.uk/pa/ld201314/ldselect/ldcomm/120/12002.htm* Department for Culture, Media and Sport, Media Ownership and Plurality: Consultation Document, 2013. Available at *https://www.gov.uk/government/consultations/media-ownership-and-plurality*

(4)   R. McChesney, *Digital Disconnect,* The New Press, 2013.

(5)   A. Arsenault and M. Castells, 'The Structure and Dynamics of Global Multi-Media Business Networks', *International Journal of Communication* 2: 707-748, 2008.

(6)   N. Fenton (ed.), *New media, old news: journalism & democracy in the digital age*, Sage, 2009. R McChesney and V. Pickard (eds) (2011) *Will the last reporter please turn out the lights*, The New Press,2011. Pew Research Centre Project for Excellence in Journalism, *The State of the News Media* 2013, available at *http://stateofthemedia.org/2013*

(7)   Ofcom, *Report on public interest test on the proposed acquisition of British Sky Broadcasting Group plc* by News Corporation, Ofcom, 2010, p13.

(8)   House of Lords Communications Committee Report on Media Plurality, p13.

Contributors

Ann Field is a former national officer with Unite/GPMU and a member of News International Dispute Exhibition and Archive group. She worked in The Times library from 1971-77 until elected as a full-time officer of the print union NATSOPA; and was a full-time officer of the clerical branch of SOGAT when 700 members of the branch were sacked by Murdoch in 1986 at the beginning of the year-long struggle. She was elected as a GPMU national official in 1998 retiring at the end of 2009. Since retirement she has resumed activity in the Campaign for Press and Broadcasting Freedom (CPBF) and has key interests in trade union rights, the history of printworkers' trade unions and struggles, and media ownership and accountability.

Des Freedman is a professor of Media and Communications at Goldsmiths, University of London. He is the author of *The Politics of Media Policy*; co-author (with James Curran and Natalie Fenton) of *Misunderstanding the Internet*; co-editor (with Michael Bailey) of *The Assault on Universities: A Manifesto for Resistance*, and co-editor (with Daya Thussu) of *Media and Terrorism: Global Perspectives*. He is particularly interested in issues of media power and media reform. He is the chair of the UK Media Reform Coalition and on the national council of the CPBF. He is an editor of the journal Global Media and Communication and his next book on The Contradictions of Media Power is being published by Bloomsbury in September 2014.

Tim Gopsill was for 21 years the elected editor of *The Journalist*, the magazine of the National Union of Journalists (NUJ). A journalist since his student days, he has worked in newspapers, magazines and radio. Active in the NUJ since the early 1970s, he was a member of its National Executive Council from 1984 to 1987. He was launch editor of the NUJ website and was responsible for matters relating to press freedom and professional standards as the official working with the union's Ethics Council. Tim was the founding secretary of the national UK Press Card Scheme in 1992 and represents the NUJ on the National Council of the Campaign for Press and Broadcasting Freedom. He edited the CPBF journal *Free Press* for four years. He is co-author of *Journalists: 100 years of the NUJ,* published by Profile Books in 2007.

Jonathan Hardy is Reader in Media Studies at the University of East London and teaches political economy of media at Goldsmiths College, London. He is the author of *Critical Political Economy of Media: An Introduction* (forthcoming); *Cross-Media Promotion* (2010) and *Western Media Systems* (2008). He writes on media, marketing communications, regulation and policy. He is Secretary of the Campaign for Press and Broadcasting Freedom.

Gary Herman has worked as a journalist and author, covering film and popular music and, more recently, information technology and new media. He has also worked as an editor and occasional lecturer and trainer. In the 1990s, he worked with trade unions, helping them to engage with the internet. He is a national council member of the CPBF and chair of the NUJ's New Media Industrial Council. Since 1999, Gary has built web sites and offered related consultancy services for trade union and not-for-profit clients. In 2007, he sat on the NUJ's Multimedia Working Commission and helped to launch the union's survey of employment in the UK media and journalism industry. In 2012, he researched and wrote a comparative review of developments in the media and journalism in France and the UK for the European Union federations for journalists and media workers.

Mike Holderness is Chair of the European Federation of Journalists Authors' Rights Expert Group and a freelance journalist. There was a day in 1990 when had had read the entire World-Wide Web (all nine pages at info.cern. ch). He was not impressed: the alternative Gopher protocol seemed like a much more rigorous way of organising information. Now he is also Chair of the Creators' Rights Alliance in the UK (*www.creatorsrights. org.uk*) and editor of www.londonfreelance.org for his NUJ branch, which includes maintaining databases of market information. In between he earns a living as a freelance science and technology writer and editor – most recently for *New Scientist* (writing and editing the 'Feedback' diary column) and for BECTU.

Paul Routledge is a *Daily Mirror* columnist and was previously political correspondent on *The Observer* and the *Independent on Sunday* and labour editor of *The Times*.

Martin Shipton is Media Wales' Chief Reporter. He joined *Wales on Sunday* in 1994, moving on to the *Western Mail* eight years later. He specialises in controversial and investigative stories and has been involved in covering the Welsh Assembly since it was established in 1999. Educated at school in London and at York and Cardiff Universities, he spent the early part of his career working for the Northern Echo in Darlington. His book on the Assembly's first decade, *Poor Man's Parliament*, was published in 2011. An NUJ activist since he was a trainee, he chairs the union's Trinity Mirror Group Chapel.

Andrew Wiard began his career in 1974 at Report of London, mentored by Simon Guttmann, one of the founding fathers of modern photojournalism, and where he later became the main Report photographer, until 1988. Since then, apart from brief periods at Select, as an archive member of Network, and as a founder of Report Digital, he has run his own show, still working in the Report tradition. He represented the NUJ on the British Copyright Council and the Committee on Photographic Copyright, campaigning for the reforms of the Copyright Designs and Patents Act 1988, was a co-founder of both the photographers email group EPUK and the copyright activists group Stop 43, which kicked the damaging copyright provisions of Clause 43 out of the Digital Economy Act 2010. He is currently on the board of the British Press Photographers' Association (BPPA) and chairs the NUJ's Photographers' Council.

Granville Williams has long-standing interests in media ownership and the role of corporate lobbying in the formation of media policy. His publications include *Britain's Media: How They Are Related*, CPBF, 2nd edition 1996. He prepared two reports for the European Federation of Journalists on European media ownership: *Threats on the Landscape* (2002) and *Eastern Empires: Foreign Ownership in Central and Eastern Europe* (2003). He is Director of the CPBF's Media Ownership in the Age of

Convergence project. His most recent book is *Settling Scores: The Media, the Police and the Miners' Strike*, CPBF, 2014.

Help us to be effective.
Join the **CPBF**

The CPBF was established in 1979 by people - mostly in the media unions - who wanted to resist the power of the corporate press and campaign for the real independence and accountability of the media.

In 1995 Tony Blair decided that the support of Rupert Murdoch was crucial to electoral success and Labour abandoned long-standing policies on media ownership. The CPBF became a lone voice challenging the orthodoxies of deregulation and liberalisation of media ownership pursued by New Labour.

We saw the stark consequences of these policies in July 2011 when Murdoch's media empire, intent on acquiring full control of the enormously profitable BSkyB, was suddenly engulfed in the phone-hacking scandal. The crisis rocked the media, police and political establishment and led to the Leveson inquiry and report.

Now politicians are rediscovering the crucial link between a diverse media and a healthy democracy, and the need to place ownership limits on big media.

If you don't think we get the media we deserve, join with us to campaign for more diverse, democratic and accountable media. We are a membership-based organisation which relies on individuals and organisations for the funds to continue to do our work. You can find out more about us and download a membership form from: http://www.cpbf.org.uk
email us at freepress@cpbf.org.uk
or write to us at CPBF, 23 Orford
Road, Walthamstow, London E17 9NL